THE SAKYANS OF SOUTH-EAST ASIA

THE SAKYANS OF SOUTH-EAST ASIA

An Introspection Of Tracing Roots

S.P. TALUKDAR

GYAN PUBLISHING HOUSE
New Delhi - 110002

The Sakyans of South-East Asia

Rs. 540

ISBN : 81-212-0878-5

Published in 2006 in India by
Gyan Publishing House
5, Ansari Road, Darya Ganj
New Delhi - 110002

Phones: 23282060, 23261060
Fax : 011-23285914
E-mail : books@gyanbooks.com

Laser Typesetting at: Mega Graphics, Delhi
Printed at: Salasar Imaging System, Delhi.

Dedicated

to

Friendly

Sakyan

Society

Contents

Foreword

Sri Sakya Prasad Talukdar has prepared a book on Buddhism which is different from other available book on the subject. It treats Buddhism from the standpoint of the people, the Sakyas, who threw up the Prince Siddharta or Gautama who ultimately became the Buddha or the Enlightened one. The book compromises of topics like ethnographic study of the Sakyas, the ethnic Buddhism in Assam, study of scripts, Buddhisattva idea, Archaeological study, DNA study etc. Intertwined in between are discussions of the life and teachings of the Buddha.

Sri Talukdar's aim is to identify the modern Sakyas, if any. Any DNA study is possible once the basic DNA traits of the Sakyas are ascertained. Therefore, the DNA study, though remarkably accurate, can properly done only at a later stage.

Sri Talukdar, basically on the migration history of Eurasia, leans on the possibility that in the Scythians perhaps lie the original roots of the Sakyas. Developing this assumption he is tempted again to identify the Koch population of Bengal and Assam as the Modern Sakyas. However, keeping the scientific temperament alive, he does not make any absolute statement. His elaboration on the state of Buddhism in the sub-continent does not have much bearing on the central theme. The discussion is interesting all the same.

Since it is a book of its own kind, it is enough if it enthuses some researchers to go deep into the problem. The loose ends of various arguments are because of the relative novelty of the problem. I wish he polishes the language before 'The Sakya's of the South-East Asia—An Introspection' is finally submitted for publication. I am confident that the book will add a new dimension, not necessarily philosophical or religious, to the study of Buddhism. I wish its wide circulation.

2 August 2005

Prof. Sibnath Sarma
Department of Philosophy
Guwahati University
Guwahati-781014, Assam
India

Preface

Though a Lotus flower grows in mud of a pond, but it dwells above water standing for purity — Buddha nature. This is the meaning of the term Buddha, Sakyamuni (566-486 BC), whose teaching still remained most evident and alive long after his mahaparinirvana. He was born in Nepal, where his father reigned over the tribe Sakyas in which he belonged. He was commonly known Gautama.

There is no much of intimate knowledge, information on Sakyas genealogy prior to Buddha's life. The term Sakya is used in India to refer Buddha's clan. Have they originated beyond India? The study of it, I find most thrilling.

There are disparate communities spreaded over a large number of countries who claim offshoots from Sakyan in which Gautamas Buddha was born. The term 'Sakyan' include them all. It is probably they belong to Scythian tribe of central Asia. Sakyan is also a generic term indicating those who joined Buddha's life (followers). The Sakyan genealogy has been dealt in the two scriptures namely, (1) Acchariyabbhuta Dharma Sutta and (2) Mahapadana Sutta, the Scythian, Iranian people with the related Pahlaves dominated north-west India from about 100 BCE to about 7 CE. They originated from Central Asia (Tarim Basin). Human beings began to arrive in India about 60,000 years ago, including nordic Aryans from Turkey, Iraq, Iran, Afghanistan and elsewhere. This infused new ideas and intermingling culture.

Buddha brought a huge transformation in social, cultural and political life in the Gangetic basin in central India, which was the intermingling of culture of another wave of people who entered through north-east passage of India. This was the Sakyan route long past. The recounting of Sakyan history is very thrilling as it round the people of India with the people of Central Asia.

A bit of information of the origin of Sakyan clan in India in the wedlock of brother and sister in the legendary history. They therefore, took pride in maintaining the purity of their family and clan.

Historically speaking, there are records to show that Sakyas were very tricky and self-respecting people. During Buddha's time King Prasenjit asked for a daughter of a Sakya chief as his wife. But the Sakyas were too weak to refuse openly to the request to a such powerful potentiate in their immediate neighbourhood, had resort to a trick. The offering of a Sakya chief by a slave girl was passed off as the legitimate daughter of the Sakya race and married to Prasenjit. A son Vidudabha was born of this marriage, and when he paid a visit to his maternal grandfather the true origin of his mother came to light. It naturally created a great sensation and Prasenjit discreted both his queen and son. But the great Buddha told him that whatever might have been the origin of the queen, the son belongs to the caste of his father and on his advice Prasenjit restored both the queen and the prince to favour. But, after having become the king Vidudabha, made a revengeful attack on Sakyas and 50,000 were massacred in a day during Buddha's life time in Kapilavastu resulting virtual alineation of Sakya clan. The name Sakya is still prevalent among a small number of people in Nepal, and Kargil in

Kashmir, India. There is a good number of them in the Chittangoang hill tracts in Bangladesh and the Arakan Yoma (hills) in Myanmar. There are two hypothetical analysis of the origin of Sakyas in India: (1) From Tibet through the Himalayan ranges of Nepal, (2) From the royal families of Benares, the most ancient city capital in India — Jamboo Deepa.

The origin of Sakya clan in India has remained unknown, but historically it is known that Sakya King, Dhaja Raja, fled away and founded a kingdom in Moriya (Kubo Valley) now in Myanmar. It is known to be the reverse journey of Sakyas to their own clan in the basin of the river Irrawadi, where Dhaja Raja married the widow of Binnakya Raja being of the same clansmen. The Sakya kingdoms in the Irrawadi valley were over ran by the Tai-Shan race from Yun-nan (China). This is the historical background of the disbursement of Sakyas in Myanmar.

In India, Sakyas are blood related with Koliyas, Buddha's mother side. The pedigree of Sakyas followed cross-cousin marriage system, under which a man's children are expected to marry his sister's children, but not his brother's children. This mode of reckoning kin is found in its typical form among Tamils, the Todas and other people of South India. Endogamy was very common among Sakyas.

The distinctiveness, characteristics and cultural traits of the Sakyas would be another determining factor of them. The progenition of Sakya race is still alive. There are a numerous group of people in the South-East Asian countries who believe to be in the genealogical line of Sakya clone. When people are spilling over from one area to another how Sakyas can be a distinctive clan? What is the origin of

Sakyas? Is there Sakyas in the present day? What is their social position in the present day? Can there be any scientific gene study to explore all the hidden inter-connectivity between communities?

As it is not known the biological clone of Sakyans, it might not be easier to ascertain it, but it must not be absolute impossibility if we systematically study it scientifically. A study is being carried out on the origin of Sakyan people who claims a common origin going backs to the time of Gautama Buddha himself. This hypothesis is being studied using genetic variations on Y-chromosome and other disciplines of knowledge like archaeology, history, genetic anthropology and that might open up light on this study. This is being carried out under the leadership of Dr. Mark. G. Thomas University College, London in collaboration with the author in collection of the mouth Swab. This research study is approved by the Joint University College, London and University College, London Hospital Committee on the Ethics of Human research (study number 99/0196).

The project aims to test claims, based on oral histories, that the Sakyan people have a common biological origin. In the first instance the molecular tools used will be polymorphic markers on the Y-chromosome. This may later be extended to using mitochondrial DNA variations.

In the US the Human Genome Diversity Project (HGDP) has been founded in 1994. It aims to reconstruct the history of human evolution, migration pattern, unidentifying the origin of the existing population without making distinction on the basis of class and race. Human population in the ancient time were small and many were isolated from each other by geographical barriers – originating the racial classifications. In recent years the non-visible characteristics of different racial groups such as blood groups, immune reactions and enzyme structures are being studied. In modern science a more relevant characteristics are being studied to trace the origin of genealogical line. The innate characteristics are also considered on intrinsic subject of study. The genetic anthropologists (scientists) have interest to trace the root of Sakyans in which Gautama Buddha was born.

Sakyamuni Buddha's last word was:

All things decay, be mindful, be righteous, be vigilant. Be the lamps unto yourself: ATMA DEEPA BHAVA

"BE THE FLAME OF YOUR OWN LIGHT"

1

Sakyan Background

Sakyamuni's historical lineage with the race of celestial beings who descended to clear the darkness in human life. The Buddha's era is reckoned from the death of Sakyamuni in Kushinara (C 486 BC). He was born in Kapilavastu (C 566 BC). There are many mystic ideas of the origin of Sakyas in India.

The early history of Central Asia is closely related to the movement of its people Scythians – the nordic Aryans and Mongoloids. In the Central Asia they are known Saka. They are frequently mentioned, in Indian literature. The history of Sakyas can be reconstructed on the basis of classical Iranian and Chinese sources. The eastern Turkistan from Pamir upto the frontier China was occupied by the nordic Aryans of different affiliations, and Saka is one of it. The history of Sakas in the north-west seems to have began in Taxila, Khotan, Pamir, Kabul, Gandhara etc.

During Sakyamuni's times' India was divided into a multitudes of big, small principalities and tribal republics. It continued till some centuries back. Kapilavastu was a Sakyan republic. At that time the people of Kasi, Kosala, Videha and Magadha were excluded from Brahma desha, the believer in Brahma means advaita (soul), identifying every soul is identical with the one the universal soul (advaita-vedanta). Sakyamuni preached non-soul (no unified subject) i.e. emptyness, Sunnyta. In Buddhism mind has to attain the unconditioned, realising the whole truth. India has become the meeting point of this two believing systems.

In the first place, we know, the term 'Hindu' was attributed to the Indians by the Iranian invaders at later stages of history (Sindu takes the form Hindu, ancient Iranian 'h' for the Indo-Aryan 's'), but the chief element of what was to become known as Hindu was well established, Casteism classification of people in 4 (four) barnas, on the basis of daily life. The perpetration of it still continues in different social dimentions.

This is the part of history relating to the western corner of India. There has been intermingling from east by waves or stream of migration of people, viz. Tibeto Burman, Mon Khamer and Tai-Chinese. They all became a diverge group of people in different geographical areas, but they might be emerging at one point of time from the same root. History suggests, different creed of people intermixed with Sakyans. The Tai-Shan from Yun-nan over ran the Sakyans.

In the first place history has recorded a number of Sakyan kings, namely:

(1) Abhi Raja (C 923 BC).

(2) Dhaza Raja (Sakyamuni's Contemporary).

(3) Binnakya Raja, who was reigning on the river basin of Irrawady (Myanmar).

The Sakyans are distinct people, in their faith and keenness at looking back to the past birth and to trace the continuity of consciousness from one life to life without break for 10 (ten) thousand aeons, Kalpas (in Pali language, a age of the world; the period beginning with the reign of a world and extending beyond its dissolution to the origin of a new world), to having divine insight to find out where the dying consciousness is born; to acquire the iddhi power (road to success in Buddhism, contemplating mind on a good object to become invisible, travel a distant land etc. Sakyan believe a person's status in the society was programmed in the past. Life's understanding comes only through self-knowledge, Buddhism deals with developing mind (insight by individual efforts through absorbtion (Jhana in Pali) of one's mind to search the highest (supreme enlightenment). Every human being is born with full potentials for developing towards this goal. Sakyamuni is also called Mahamuni, an ancient of which was at Babbootoung in Arakan.

Sakyamuni is said to have given 84,000 teachings something for everyone. It is indeed directed to explain in this manner—each nomad started with four elements in combination with other life, nomads, which were collectively expressed as different living organisms, they separately and collectively passed through a series of 84,000 graded birth. It looks like a legend, but how wonderful, it would appear, if we turn in scientific analysis. Science had made measure that the age of the world is 13 million years, while human beings originated just 2.3 million years back only. At that time a huge energy exploded and transformed into four elements (air, water, earth and heat). Human beings is an energy which changes shapes (transforms) from one shape to another. There are numerous transformations in human life.

The earliest settlers in Myanmar are known to be Thek (Sak, in local language 'Th' is pronounced as 'Sa' who were probably Sakyan origin. There are different clansmen in this tribe. There is another reference to a Chinese work of 6th century AD, called a history of southern princes by the author Yang-Tasi of Chen-Tufu in the province of Sze-chem which traces the descend of prince Chiu-Lung from Asoka of Magadha (264-228 B C) in direct line. This legend of Asoka showing relationship between the ruling dynasties of Yun-nan (China) and Magadha (India).

It also emerged that silk for instance was first invented in the present Sichuan province in China, Kautilya an Indian Statesman in the 4th century BC was the first non-Chinese author to record in his *Arthashastra* (principle of economy) about the Chinese silk cocoon (Kauseya) and silk bundles (cina patta). Scholars suspect that during this time–or even earlier–there was brisk traffic between Sichuan and Magadha (Kautilya's country) through Yun-nan via Assam and Manipur. In the 3rd century BC the philosophy of Buddhism came into contact with the Greek and Parthian ideals. The most essential part of Buddhist history is afar away from the present geographical area of India in the east and west directions. There were different waves of people including the Manipuris who originated from Yun-nun, China. In the earlier days, it was a state whose Suzernity once reigned from Kubo valley (now in Myanmar) to Surma valley in Assam (India). In Kubo valley was originally a part of India, but it was gifted to Myanmar in 1953. Kubo valley is a continuous to Chandel district of Manipur. The British gifted it to Myanmar in 1834.

The King Kanishka was ruling over the western India in 125 AD. He was a Sakyan wearing an Iranian tunic with a Scythian cap on his head and a nomadic horseman's heavy boot on his feet. In the 3rd century Kushan empire was overthrown by the Iranian invaders. It also created an upheaval on races in Kashmir (north India). By this time Buddhism had made a significant progress in India and China making communication between nations open.

In those days the state Magadha (now Bihar) was dominated by Dravidians, Mongoloid comprising of Mundas, Santhals, Marmas and Arakanese now in Myanmar, with the growing of time they became divided people extending over the south Bihar, West Bengal, Orissa and a large part of north Bihar which included eastern and north Bengal which was the home of the Cooch (Koch), a Scythian origin. They played a variety of roles when Gaur (present Malda) was the capital of ancient Bengal, Koch-Mandi was an important resting place while travelling in the direction eastern countries Coch-Bihar (now in North Bengal and western Assam were under the Coch kingdom. Before the ancient capital had become Hindu metropolis of Bengal, it could probably a place dominated by Scythians who were all related to one another as having originated from one place long past.

History reveals that it was also a fact to note the Tibetan traditions dwelled on the bank of Bhagirathi (Ganges), a fact that could probably to a Turanian Sovereign resident at Gaur.

The people in the Indian sub-continent had grown up since long past from Bahujan (varied identities), majority of them claiming to be from the Sakyan line in which Sakyamuni Gautama was born. They are now termed as Dalits. In Tamil language the word Pariah and Sakya are syonym means untouchable caste. The author of the famous classic book 'The Thirukural' was a Pariah and the book is the epitome of 'Tripitaka' sacred religious book of The rovada Buddhist (The busket of discipline– Vinaya Pitaka: the busket of discourses – Sutta Pitaka; and the busket of Philosophy – Abhidharma Pitaka). Some say these Pitakas were first recorded in writing from memory by the wise priests in the reign of Vattagamani whose reign dated 88 to 76 B C.

A Sakyan clan called Lichavis of north Bihar extended power to the south across the Ganges and to have occupied ancient capital Pataliputra (now Patna). A local Hindu chief who bore the honoured name Chandra Gupta married a Lichavi princes and established the Gupta era. The limit of the empire was extended to the east bank of the mighty Brahmaputra which is called Tsangpo in Tibet. This is how the movement of people followed along the river line.

In the history there was an important Buddhist Cultural Centre by name "Champa". But it could not be identified distinctly as yet. According to Archaeologists it was south of Bhagalpur in Bihar comprising of present Santhal Parganas and Bhirbhum. There is another place called Tsampanynago sounds like Champa which was centre of Sakya line in Myanmar. It is situated at the mouth of small river flows from Mogout and Kyetpen joining into the Irrawadi river in Myanmar.

According to the records of Chinese travelled Fa-Hien (406 AD) and Hiuen-Tsang (643 AD), majority of people were Buddhist in India in those days. Hiuen-Tsang travelled India inquest of knowledge and to find the truth of India's excellence. Hiuen-Tsang was treated with royal honour by Harshavardhan at Kanauj on the Ganges for the exaltation of Mahayana (Bodhisattva for benefiting all living creatures) founded by Nagarjuna about 56 B C). Hiuen-Tsang was a teacher in Nalanda Buddhist university till he went back to China in 641 AD. He was a Mahayanist preacher.

Bodhisattva for benefiting all living creatures, greater vehicle of the school of Buddhism, founded by Nagarjuna about 56 B C. Hiuen-Tsang was a teacher in Nalanda university, and himself was a Mahayanist preacher.

Buddhism had undergone slow decadence from 9th century, when Pal dynasty rose to power, formerly known as Anga and gradually extended its sway over the whole of Bihar and north Bengal. Traces of their rule are very common in the south of Dinajpur (Bengal), where the memory of Mahipal, in particular, is preserved both in traditions of the people and in numerous names of places, like the kings of Pundra, they were Buddhists, but they were tolerant towards Hindus. They were driven away from Bengal proper about the middle of eleventh century, by a king named Vijaya Sen, of the Sen family, but continued to rule for some time longer in Bihar. The Sen rose to power in Bengal towards the end of 10th century from the Mahananda and Bhagirathi and the west to the Karatoya and the Brahmaputra on the east. At that time there appeared Sen dynasty who where Hindus and during their rule Buddhism was actively discouraged.

Attempts for revival of Buddhism by Palas in Magadha, but the fall of that kingdom resulted in acceleration the process of destruction. No process for revival of Buddhism could be made. Finally, the last of this line was defeated in 1197 AD by Muhammad-i-Bakhtyar Khilji (a Turki), where soldiers destroyed the capital of Odantapuri and massacred the Buddhist monks assembled there.

The decrement of Buddhism began by the major development of Hindu philosophy by Sankaracharya in 788-850 AD which resulted a big surge of Hinduism. Buddhism was disbanded and many of them were driven out moving beyond Assam and Bengal in rugged country covered with dense forest and underwood between Arakan Yoma and Chittagong with ranges of hills. The earliest inhabitants perpetuated a string of ties with Sakyan in which Gautama Buddha was born. Therefore, it served as a sanctuary of Buddhists when they became victims of radical Hindus and Muslims. History records; Buddhism is a living religion in Chittagong proper, in the hill tracts, and in Tippera. It was introduced in these districts about the 9th century A D direct from Magadha, when the eastern provinces of Bengal in Chittagong, was under the sway of a Rajput prince named Gopi Pala. The Mahayana Buddhism, which about that time prevailed in Magadha and Tibet, was preached in Chittagong by Bengali Buddhists. In the 10th century AD Chittagong, in a manner, became the centre of the Buddhism in Bengal. In 13th century, it was a mixed population of Buddhists and Hindus. In 17th century Mughals extended their conquest to Chittagong and then came the British colonial rule, which later made it a part of Muslim homeland. The ethnic tribal Buddhist became broken people and lost their homeland.

Will the long drawn dispute over the location of Buddha's birthplace end in favour of Nepal...? The area around Tilaurakot (Nepal) crowded with unexcavated or partly excavated Buddhist sites. About 65 archaeological sites have been identified and the authorities want to develop at least seven. The remains of the Eastern Gateway of Kapilavastu (At Tilaurakot) through which Gautama Buddha is believed to have walked out at night.

A century-old dispute over the location of Kapilavastu, where Prince Siddarth (late Gauthama, the Buddha) grew up, is about to end in favour of Tilaurakot in Nepal, and not Piprahawa, India. "Tilaurakot is situated on the Banganga which is thought to have been called Bhagirathi by the Sakyans", said Prof. Tulsi Ram Baidya, Chairman of the Nepal History Association. "There is no river near Piprahawa".

Tilaurakot's claim to Kapilavastu is based primarily on four areas of irrefutable evidence. The place is a derivative not of the name of Kapila, the saga, but an oil producing shrub in Nepalese called Kapila, which is used for medicinal and cooking purposes from time immemorial by the Nepalese, Tilaurakot too means 'tell' or oil and 'kot' field of sesame (dil). Firstly, according to Buddhist literature, Kapilavastu was situated on a river which was called Bhagirathi. It was a common term used to identify all rivers in the area as Bhagirathis (blessed rivers) that finally unite with the holy Ganges or Ganga.

Secondly, a capital city would have fortified as there were royal feuds among them then as now between the kingdoms or the people of the country. Prof. Baidya, reiterated, "We can still see remnants of a moat and walls at the site of Tilaurakot site. The walls are 10 feet wide. Unless it was a capital city, it could not have had walls. The area of Kapilavastu is around 1,700 feet by 1,300 ft. It was too huge for a monastic complex".

Thirdly, Japanese and Nepalese archaeologists later found painted grey ware in a third century trench dug by Debala Mitra, the archaeologist. In the Indian subcontinent painted grey ware was in existence as far back as the eleventh century BC, suggestive of the fact this site was inhabited even earlier than that.

Fourthly, a huge collection of coins had been excavated at Tilaurakot, which too is direct evidence that there was a palace at site with a royal treasury, and not a monastic complex.

As regards Piprahawa, the Nepalese archaeologists and others contend, it could have been an area under Sakyan rulers and the site of a monastery.

The Buddha speaking about Himself declared, "I am a Khattiya, warrior-noble stock. I was reborn into a Khattiya family. I am a Gotama by clan. My lifespan is of short length, it is brief and soon over, one who lives long now completes the century or a little more.... A king, Suddhodana by name, was my father. A queen, Maha Maya by name, was the mother that bore me. The royal capital was the city of Kapilavastu". (Digha Nikaya 14. Condensed translation by late Ven. Bhikkhu Nanamoli's 'The Life of the Buddha'). On the Maha Parinirvana of the Buddha (passing away) at Kusinara, several kings and rulers of principalities claimed relics to be enshrined in their countries. The Sakyans of Kapilavastu too staked their claims saying, "The Blessed One was the greatest of our blood, we too are worthy of a share of the Blessed One's bones. We too will build a monument and hold a ceremony" (Ibid, page 331). In these times the present Piprahawa too was in the kingdom of Kapilavastu, and the presently excavated site could be the place of the monastery and monument Sakyans built.

Presently Tilurakot is a mass of excavated and unexcavated sites, coming under Nepal. Birendra K. Yadav, the Project Manager of Lumbini Development Trust says: "We want to develop at least seven sites. The first of course is Tilaurakot, the site of Kapilavastu and the others are Gotihawa, Kudan, Niglihawa, Arourakot, Sagarahawa and Sisania".

The search for Kapilavastu emerged when James Princeps deciphered the Brahmi and Kharosnti scripts in the 18th century and learned of a plethora of rock and pillar edicts based on Buddhist scriptural writings. Prof. Lassen studied Buddhist literature and wrote in 1858 that the town of Kapilavastu should be on the banks of the Rohin, which was identified as ancient river Rohini in Gorakhpur district of Uttar Pradesh.

Archaeology proper started in India in 1861 with Sir Alexander Cunningham surveying north India.

Cunningham vs Coningham

Cunningham reading the accounts of the two Chinese pilgrim monks located Kapilavastu at 80 miles southeast of Sravasti, which again he located at the desolate Set Mahet near Balrampur in Gonda district. He learnt of a town called Nagar Khas, eight miles southeast in Basti district and surmised it to be Kapilanagara, a corruption of the name Kapilavastu. He was dead certain and never cared to excavate the place and lost no time in writing his 'Ancient Geography of India'. His assistant Carlleyle followed him in 1876. Having not seen ruins a set Mahet, Carlleyle proceeded a further 18 miles and reached Bhuilatal, with a plethora of brick mounds on the banks of the river Rawai. His senior concurred with him.

Historically it is apparent that Hindu Rana rulers of Nepal did not permit foreigners to dig in Nepal. Only excavations that were done were in British India and what was concluded by them came to be accepted without a murmur as the total truth. However, in Nepal things changed for the better with the ruling Rana's brother, General Khadga Sumsher J.B. Rana at the end of the 19th century, himself an amateur archaeologist, invited Dr. Alois Anton Fuhrer, a German archaeologist working for the British in India to conduct excavations in Nepal territory. Further knew for certain from the Buddhist literature that Kapilavastu was never as flat as the Indian Terai and he investigated further north and located the Asokan pillar, with its fallen horse capital as accounted for by the Chinese pilgrim duo in their travel notes and declared the place as Lumbini.

Without depending much on the Chinese accounts Fuhrer, studied the Buddhist literature and suggested Kapilavastu should have been on the banks of Rohini.

He identified Rohini with Jamur flowing past Tilaurakot. He located three Asokan pillars too there. The British Indian government despatched P.C. Mukherjee to Nepal to locate the exact place of Kapilavastu. He fixed it to be at Tilaurakot. Historian Vincent Smith too concurred with the identification.

Tilaurakot remained the accepted Kapilavastu for six decades until Nepal invited Debala Mitra of the Archaeological Survey of India (ASI) in 1961 to excavate Tilaurakot. Her excavations revealed (northwestern trench), 'the site does not go beyond the third century BC and the capital of Kapilavastu remains to be located'. Mukherjee's findings were adjudged by her as of the seventh century A C.

Mitra's findings and conclusion were in collision with the views of other Indian archaeologists. K.M. Srivastava now dug up Piprahawa in Basti district and said that the Sakyans capital was at Piprahawa. There was little love lost between India-Nepalese archaeologists and Nepal then invited Japanese archaeologists. In 1967 Japanese-trained Nepalese archaeologists excavated the Western gateway at the Tilaurakot site and found two stupas to the north of the mound. The Japanese dug up a part of a structure believed to be King Suddhodana's palace. Terracotta with the legend Sa-ka-na-sya meaning 'the token belonged to the Sakya' and dated it to second-fifth century B.C. These excavations have now brought forth around 3,000 coins datable to the 5th century B C. The Nepalese thereafter argued that Piprahawa was only an outpost of Kapilavastu and monastery complex and Kapilavastu city proper was and is Tilaurakot. These excavations resulted in tracing painted grey pottery of the 5th-6th centuries the time of the Buddha.

On these irrefutable evidence Nepal approached UNESCO to get Tilaurakot - Kapilavastu to be declared a World Heritage Site. The UNESCO sent Dr. Robin

Coningham of Bradford University in the UK. Coningham commenced work on the site in 1997, along with Dr. Armin Schmidt and Kosh Acharya.

"During our first season at Tilaurakot in 1997, we created a topographical survey of the city and also conducted geographical survey of parts of the site. While no structures were visible on the surface, once the geographical survey data was processed, it was possible to identify the line of a major street running from the eastern gateway. This street was some seven metres wide and it was possible that further sub-divisions had been made by smaller streets at right angles, defining blocks of housing in between. As our survey was likely to have only recorded the final phase of occupation, it is most probable that we have identified the city layout of the first millennium A C", said Coningham.

Coningham's team had collected 15 carbon samples which are now being tested in Oxford University. Coningham said: "We fully expect them to confirm our early dating of the site."

Tilaurakot, emergence to its natural fame of Kapilavastu, the city where Prince Siddartha grew up, means, India will lose heavily the Japanese yen and the dollars that come from tourists. (Source: 'Soul Proprietor' R. Prasanna and Jon Stock, of The Week and English publication of Kerala, India).

2. Interpretation of Sakyan (Scythian)

As Sakya corresponds to our term Scythian; some have even thought the Saka dominions in India, which from the second to the end of the fourth century covered much of western India, may have been a major contributor to the Indianization of much of South-East Asia.

Nicholas Tarling : The Cambridge History of South-East Asia, Vol. I.

3. Sakas Sakys, Scythians

Early history of Central Asia 'The Sakas are frequently mentioned in Indian literature. They are one of the groups of Scythians. It is proposed by A.K. Narain that makes led a separate Saka group directly to Taxila from the north, passing from Khotan over the Pamirs and Indus Kohistan—an arduous route called that of the 'Hanging Pass' by Chinese chronicles (The Indo-Greeks, Oxford, p. 136). Hambly considers this suggestion fantastic. The proposes that makes began his career as a commander of Saka mercenaries in the service of the late Indo-Greek kings. With the Indo-Greek princes divided and Saka invaders at the gates, such a personage would be well placed to assume sovereign power (op. cit., p. 41). According to Sten-Konow, he was the 'first Saka emperor in India (op. cit. p. xi).

Source : B.N. Puri, Buddhism in Central Asia Motilal Banarsidass (p. 35) 1987.

4. *Dr. B.S. Guha and many other scholars are of the opinion that the ancient language of Vedas (Hindus) are highly influenced by 'Nordic Aryan' language Nordic Aryan were also inhabited in Tibet (Tribispira).*

5. Saka (Scythian)

Oriental and the Occidental world, the role of the peoples of this region in the history of Asia and Europe also deserves consideration. In fact, this participation has been the result of a long series of migrations and invasions carried out by the warring tribes claiming Central Asia as their homeland through the ages. From earliest times Central Asia had at least two distinct and separate racial and linguistic groups, called the Scythians and the Huns. The former are supposed to belong to the 'Great White Race', speaking an Aryan or Indo-European language. The Huns, however, belonged to the 'Great Yellow Race' with a good deal of Mongoloid blood, and speaking a language different from the former and generally termed as Turanian or Ural-Altaic. The Scythian or Indo-European element in the population of Central Asia was dominant in the region now called Turkestan and it was here that the members of this group, pressed by political as well as economic forces, spread outward in all direction. The Scythian migrations had greater impact upon the regions to the south of Turkestan, sweeping over the Persian Plateau and into North-Western India where they settled down permanently, shaking off their nomadic norms and habits. Those Scythians left in Turkestan, however, retained their nomadic habits and were not slow to invade their kinsmen to the south, leading to permanent conquest and occupation. The Scythian group in Parthia ruled there for nearly five centuries, establishing political control over the agricultural population of the Persian Plateau. The position in North-West India (now Pakistan) was, however, different with several Scythian groups ruling one after another.

Source : B.N. Puri, Buddhism in Central Asia, by Motilal Banarsidass, 1987, p. 8.

6. Sakyan Origin (History)

In the third century, Iranian invaders encroached upon an eventually overthrew the Kushan empire. As they appear to have done in Northern India, these Iranian tolerated and even encouraged the continuation of Buddhism in Western Central Asia. Some of the most impressive Buddhist ruins of Western Central Asia–such as the great rock-hewn Buddha at Bamian and the Jaulian stupa at Taxila–date from these post-Kushan age. In Eastern Central Asia the fall of Kushan empire left the way open for the prosperous independence of several mercantile city states along the northern and southern branches of the Silk Road skirting the Takla Makan desert. Among these, Khotan in the south, Ashgar in the west and Kucha and Turfan in the north were pre-eminent, because of their reliance upon trade, these cosmopolitan city states tolerated a variety of religions, including Zoroastrianism, Mithraism, Hinduism and Christianity. For most of the first millennium, however they were primarily Buddhist.

In the fifth century the same ferocious Huns who destroyed the Gupta dynasty in India did a great damage to Buddhism in western central Asia as well as in Kashmir. Muslim invaders began to dominate western Central Asia from eight century. Nevertheless, Buddhism appears to have survived in the reign until about one thousand C E.

Source : Buddhism (A History) by Noble Ross, published by Asian Humanities Press, USA.

7. The Burmans (Abhiraja, Dhaza Raja)

The affinities of the Burmese with the Himalayan languages are unmistakable, and, though the evidence on the point is almost wholly linguistic, the theory that the Tibetan and the Burmese races have a common origin has now obtained universal acceptance. The theory till recently held has been that Tibet was the early habitat of the Burman's forefathers. From a note on the Indo-Chinese language family which I have received from Dr. Grierson, however, I learn that the more correct view is that put foreword by Professor E. Kuhn of Munich in his Ueber die Herkunft und Sprache der transgang etischen Völker, namely, that western China, between the upper courses of the Yang-tse-kiang and the Hoang-ho, was the original home of the Indo-Chinese race, and that this region and not Tibet was the starting point of the Burman's migrations. According to Professor Kuhn theory the Tibeto-Burman race moved westwards from the starting point at a comparatively recent era towards the head-waters of the Irrawaddy and the Chindwin, and there divided up into separate branches, some of which maintained their westerly course, to find an ultimate resting place in Tibet and portions of Assam, while the others either worked southwards into what is now Myanmar or remained to people the country in the neighbourhood of this parting of the way.

Ref: C.C. Lowis Census of India, 1901, Vol. XII (Burma).

8. Sakyan Capital in Burma (Abhi Raja, Daza Raja)

Sakyan capital was at Tagaung in the upper river Irrawaddy 60 miles below Bhamo, founded by Abhiraja about 500 B C. We can however discover no details how long he had been there the commencement of his historical period. One blood group of the Sakyans reached in Arakan, who breaking off from the main Burmese body, probably during the period when Tagong was the Burmese capital, crossed over to Arakan Yoma and settled down on the shores of the Bay of Bengal, thus, penetrating into a region west of that occupied by the western Tibeto-Burmans.

Source : Lowis C.C. Tribes of Burma.

9. Sakyan Background

The Sakya king: Abhi Raja (1923 B C), the ancient king of Sakya. Dhaja Raza, a contemporary of Buddha who married the widow of Binakkya Raza of Burma. They were admixture with Shans who were originally from China Sakyas are blood related with Koliyas, origin of Buddha's mother.

Source : Buddha and Buddhism—Burma (The life and legend of Gautama), Rangoon by Bigendt (P.A.).

10. The Sakyan Kingdom

Then there was, at the time of Gautama Buddha, a fresh accession of immigrants from India under Daja Raja, and sixteen kings succeeded him. But for the whole fifty-one of them, little more is recorded than the length of their reigns.

It seems clear that Tagaung (Sakyan kingdom) was

dominated by the surrounding shuns, from/ Möng Maw and later from Möng Kawng (the modern Mogaung), as well as from the east, and perhaps still more by successive waves of Kachins.

The last king of the Kan Raja-Nge line, Bneinaka, was over thrown and expelled by the invasion of Tribes called Tarok and Taret, from Gandalarit which, no doubt, is the modern Chinese province of Yun-nan and the invader were Tai or shans. Consequently they divided themselves.

The Kapilavastu king Gautama himself, was not an Indian of the present day. The Burman is bloodbrother of the Buddhist races of India, before the arrival of the Aryans who expelled Buddhism from India. There were no Punjabi, Muhamedans or Bengalees in the country in the time of Suddhodana and Yasodhara and Siddartha. The Sakyan we may conclude, were Aryan, but the bulk of the population was Dravidian.

The Pyu, the Kankan and the Sak may very well have been simply wanderers from adjacent tracts, and were blood relations without knowing it.

They all amalgamated to form the Mranma.

Source : Sir J.G. Scott (1924): Burma from the Earliest time to the present day.

11. Buddhist Terminology

Iddhi: Ariya Iddhi i.e., power, ability, capacity, potentiality etc.

It constitutes six kinds of spiritual power:

(i) The power of determination (adhithan iddhi);

(ii) The power of transformation (vikubbana);

(iii) The power of spiritual creation (manomaya) i.e., the power of letting proceed from this body to another mentally proceed body;

(iv) The power of penetrating knowledge (nana vipphara), the power of inherent insight to remain unhurt in danger;

(v) The power of penetrating concentration (samadhi vipphara), producing the same result;

(vi) Noble power (ariya-iddhi) is the power of controlling one's ideas in such a way that one may consider something not repulsive as repulsive (hateful), and something repulsive as not repulsive, and remain all the time imperturable (always remaining calm) and full of equanimity.

12. Dha-Gnya-Wati (Mahamuni)

The city Dha-gnya-wati on the west bank of Ga-tsha-ba river now Kolodan in Arakan was reigned by the king Ang-dza-na, the son the king of Kapi-la-wat of Ma-ga-dha and one of these race fifty five kings reigned throughout a period of 1800 years, another dynasty then succeeded, which numbered twenty-four kings whose reign extended throughout a period of 835 years. Then came the king Tsan-da-thaoo-vee-ya, who was not of a different dynasty but in his reign Budh Gautama, having been born in Magadha, visited Arakan. The pious king in honour of him built the famous temple of Mahamuni, which still exists. The ruins of the ancient temple of Mahamuni built entirely of stone. The sites of former cities shown by the remains of tanks and ruin pagodas, the extensive stonewalls at the old capital, certainly tell of a more flourishing kingdom then what British founded.

Source : Phayrer Journal Asiatic Society call no: 16881, Harvey, 1824, British Rule in Burma, Vol. 10, Part 2, pages 679-712.

13. Babbootoung

The old city of Arakan, which stands at the head of an interior branch of the Kuladyne, about 50 miles from Akyab, may be reached from the later place in two tides by light vessels or boats. The principle creek near the Babbootoung Hills throws off two branches, which run through the down and are crossed by lofty wooden bridges, a good deal out of repair. On the southern side of the principle street which runs east and west, are the ruins of the ancient place, and fort, consisting of a triple square enclosure of stone and brickwall, well cemented with lime, the stone having apparently kin originally employed in the construction and the subsequent repair effected with brick; the work all together is of considerable extent; and the labour bestowed in connecting the different detached hills by curtains of stones and brickwall, must have been immense. They are now, however, in a most dilapidated state, and as sites more favourably authorities of the province, it can never be an object of importance to repair eight to ten thousand, and they consist principally of old families of respectability, who continue attached to the spot from local association.

Source : Report on the eastern frontier India, 1835 by Captain R. Boileau Pemberton. Republished by the Dept. of Historical and Antiquarian Studies, Government of Assam, Guwahati.

14. The Origin of Sak

Kadu is spoken in the neighbouring district of Myitekyina, Katha, and upper Chindwin, and Ganan in the last two of these. Ganan is merely a variant of Kadu, and its speakers as well as those of Kadu call themselves 'A Sak'. This leads us to Tibet, spoken far away, in the Akyab district, which is allied to Kadu. Mr. Taylor tells us that, according to Burmese history in early days the Saks inhabited the upper part of the Irraway Valley. Some of these are supposed to have travelled from their original settlement in north Burma in a south–westerly direction into Arakan. He suggests that some of them may have passed to Manipur and become the ancestors of the Andro and Sengmai tribes. Another possible explanation is however that the original Kadu-Saks, while still in north Burma spread also into Manipur, and that the Andro Sengmai were left behind there, like the Kadus of Myithyina and the neighbourhood, when the Saks migrated to the south-west. The fact that there were servile tribe, and that they were expropriated by the Meitheis show that they must have been early settlers there, and that they were found thereby the Meitheis when they conquered the country.

Finally, Daingnet is the language, much corrupted by the Indo-Aryan Bengali, of the descendants of Sak prisoners of war from the Valley of lower Chindwin, who were captured by king Mindi of Arakan at the close of the thirteenth century and made to settle in the Akyab District.

Source : Motilal Banarsidass, Linguistic Survey of India, Vol. I, Part I, Daingnet (Sak), 1927, 1973.

15. Historical Background of Maurya (Kubo Valley)

Dhaja Raja (Sakya King) fled towards the east and first founded a kingdom in Maurya. The place named Maurya is from the Mauryas of Pipphalivana. Maurya occurs in the Buddhist literature, such as Dhammapada. In Gautama Purana it is called Moranga in the Arakan Chronicle it is mentioned as Maurin and now it is Maurin. Maurya is also the classic name of Kubo Valley and there is also the Maurya a metropolis of Ptolemy. Maurya, as Col. Burney tells us from Burmese history, preceded Tagoung at the seat Sakya kings (See Col. Burney in Journal Asiatic Society of Bengal, Vol. 163) Maurya is now known as Mauryan (A Brumese form), according to Yele, and is a town not far south from Bhamo. Probably Dhaja Raja's first kingdom was in the Kubo Valley and Mauryan was its capital and the second kingdom in Thintwe in the Tagaung country. Maurya, after the name of the ruling clan, was perhaps another city south of Bhamo. The occurrence of this place name indicates that not only the

Sakyas but also the Mauryas came to Burma and built cites. The Mauryas belonged to a Himalayan clan like much other peoples as the Lichabis of North Bihar and Nepal with their gradual absorption in the Brahmanical society, they claimed the status Kshatryas although orthodox Brahmanists regard them as no better than sudras.

Source : The Publication Division, New Delhi, 1957, III.

16. Sakya, Dalit and Buddhist Identities

Some people deny that the independent Sakyan/ Dalit identity and try to merge with Hindu, Indian, Dravidian, Tamil, Maharashtrian, Telugu, Shudra or Bahujan identities. They have a fear of Brahminical and Shudra Hindu forces. They join with the Hindu tones, which criticize Sakyan/ Dalit leaders, activists and movements as sectarian and narrow-minded. They do not realize that the Hindus, but not Sakyans/ Dalits divided the India as a caste Hindu village and the Dalit ghetto.

Sakya/ Dalit is not a caste. Sakyans/ Dalits are not untouchables. They are an independent racial, religious, ethnic and social group that is different from the Hindus. Mangs, Chamars, Mahars, Madhigas, Malas, Pariyars and Pallars may be out-castes or scheduled castes. Untouchables may be those who believe themselves, as they are untouchables, by birth and part of Hindus. The Adi-Shudras and Harijan identities were accepted by people who depend the Hindus (Brahmins to Shudras) for political survival.

Dalit identity emerged out of awareness and knowledge. Dalits become aware that they are not untouchables but they are oppressed and the untouchability is imposed on them. The Dalits are never Hindus. They are descendant of Sakyas. The Sakyas were neither Kshatriyas not Vaisyas. They were outsider of Hindu Varna system and were original Buddhist. Buddhist culture were prevailed, the original Buddhist

(Dalits) were labourers, rulers, teachers and preachers etc. and the Indian society was highly prosperous and glorious.

Buddhism was defeated by the cunningness or Brahmins and the stupidity of Shudras who are brain and muscle powers of Hinduism. Consequently Hindus suppressed the original Buddhists due to the ideological political and social conflicts between Hindus and Buddhists. The Buddha and other Samanas (Dalit Saints) were mentioned as devils and Untouchables by Hindu scriptures. Hindus treated the Magadha as Untouchable region, Magadhi or Pariyati or Pali as untouchables' language and Buddhist literature as untouchables literature. Finally the language (Pali), the culture (Buddhist), the religion (Buddhism), the tradition (Samanic), the literature (Pali) were suppressed and destroyed.

The original Buddhists lost their own identity, language, culture, religion, status and power and became broken people. They were made to live in outside of Hindu villages and live in very degraded life. Due to the fall of righteousness (Dhamma), not only the original Buddhist fell down, but also the whole Indian sub-continent became deteriorated.

In the modern era due to the arrival of British missionaries, modern education and scientific development, and constant struggles the condition of Dalit is changing.

They realize what they are and what are their original race, language, culture, religion and tradition. They realized that they were homogeneous and indigenous people of the ancient India and were made broken people by the Hindu invaders. Since 1891, when Thatha Rettai Malai Srinivasan started a Dalit organization (Pariyar Mahajana Sabha), the Dalits were hunting for a single identity to unit all Dalits who are labeled in different names.

Bodhisatta Iyothi Thass stressed Sakya identity in 1890s and1900. He founded Sakya Buddhist Society in 1890s.

All Adi Movements such as Adi-vasi, Adi-Dravida, Adi-Tamil, Adi-Andhra, Adi-Dharmi, Adi-Hindu, Adi-Karnataka and other Dalit movements were very much interested to trace a single historical, racial, linguistic, ethnic and social identity to Dalits who are scattered in different part of Indian sub-continent. In 1920s and 1930s all India depressed class conventions stressed a single identity for Dalits. Bodhisatta Ambedkar used the word Dalit for so-called untouchables or depressed class to mean all the broken people.

Dalit panthers' movement further popularized it but the word was only confined in Maharashtra in 1970s. The Dalits are united under one identity, at least, after constant struggle of nearly one century (1891-1991). This was materialized in 1991, when the celebrations of Bodhisatta Ambedkar's birth centenary were taken place all over India.

The Dalit identity, assertion, struggles for liberation was widespread all over India in last decade (1991-2000). They could even able to carry their issue to the United Nations, the superior body of the world.

Buddhists and Dalits are not contradictory identities rather they are complementary to each other. Dalits are the descendant of ancient original Buddhist and never been part of Brahmanical Hinduism. Taking initiation (Dhiksha) or refuge (Caranam) is not conversion from any other religion to Buddhism rather it is very necessary for every Buddhist to take formal initiation and refuge and follow the path scrupulously.

The Dhamma Diksha taken by Bodhisatta Ayothidass in 1891, Bodhisatta Ambedkar in 1956, and Upasaka Udit Raj in 2001, and their followers were not incidences of conversion but, a self-proclamations of the religious identity of Dalits.

The liberation of Dalit is depending on the revival of their ancient religion (the Dhamma), ancient culture (the Sakyan sculpture), ancient tradition (the Samana tradition), ancient language (Pali/ Sakya nirutiya), and ancient identity (Sakyas).

Metta
Sakya
May all beings be happy.

17. Hivuen-Tsang's Travel

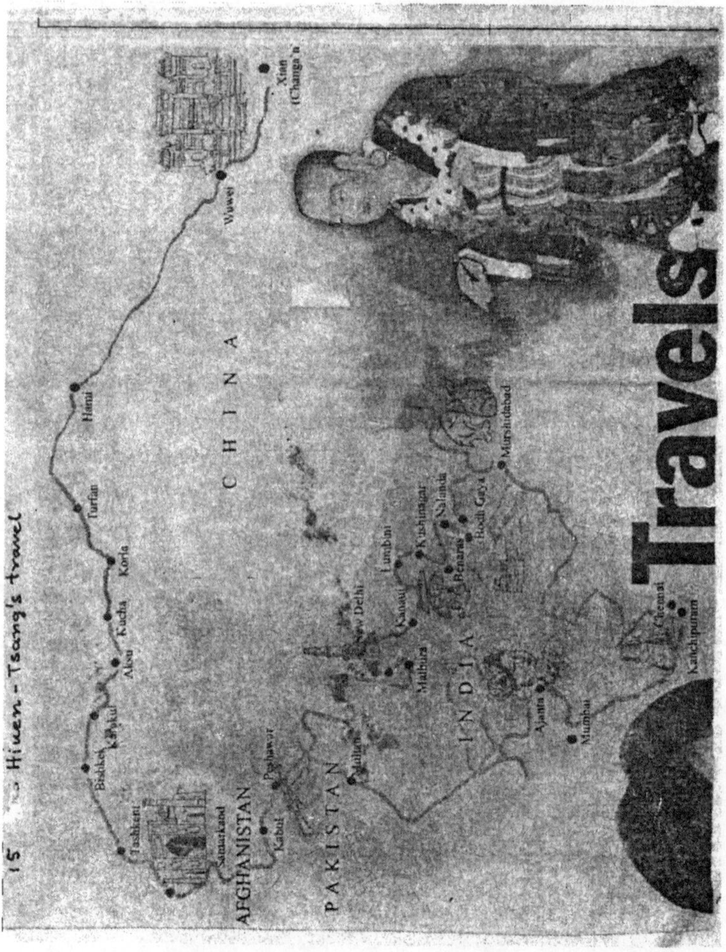

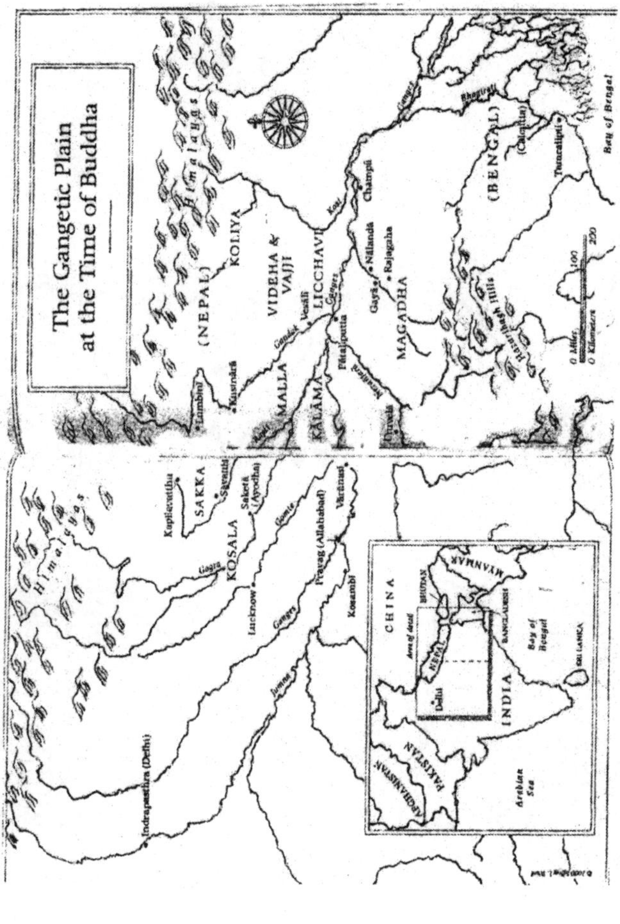
The Gangetic Plain
at the Time of Buddha
Himalayas
(NEPAL)
KOLIYA
VIDEHA & VAJJI
LICCHAVI
MALLA
KALAMA
MAGADHA
(BENGAL)
SAKKA
KOSALA
Lumbini
Kusinārā
Vesāli
Pātaliputta
Nālandā
Rajagaha
Gayā
Champā
Kapilavatthu
Sāvatthi
Lucknow
Kosambi
Vārānasī
Prayag (Allahabad)
Indrapastha (Delhi)
Ganges
Gandak
Gogra
Gomti
Jumna
Kosi
Bay of Bengal
CHINA
INDIA
NEPAL
BHUTAN
MYANMAR
PAKISTAN
AFGHANISTAN
BANGLADESH
SRI LANKA
Arabian Sea

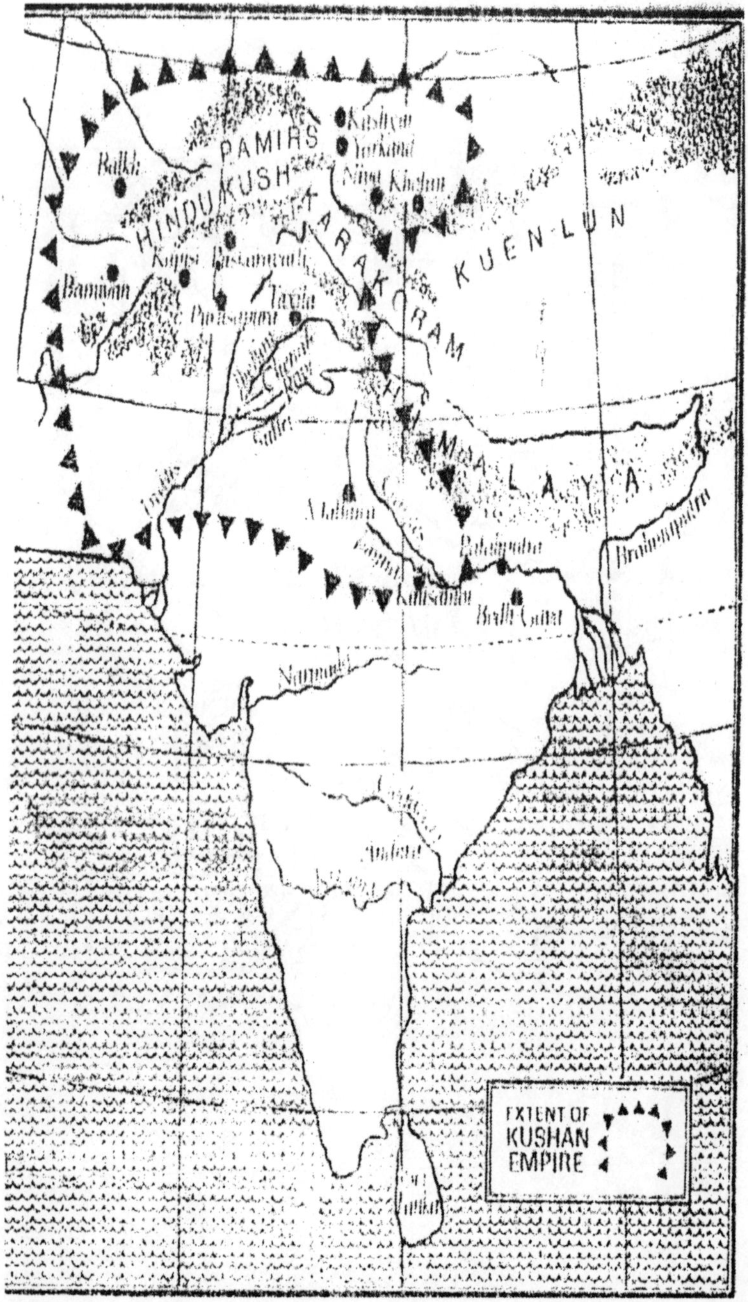
PAMIRS
HINDU KUSH
KARAKORAM
KUEN-LUN
EXTENT OF
KUSHAN
EMPIRE

2
Enthographical Anthropological

The phenomena of elements of custom, belief and relationship of China and India is most significant in most of the south–eastern Asian countries viz Afghanistan, Bangladesh, Bhutan, India, Korea, Japan, Nepal, Sri Lanka, Thailand, Iran, Indonesia, Philipines, Myanmar, Laos, Vietnam, Cambodia, Sumatra, Java and Malaysia. Their genealogical link might be more important than their religious link. As it is noticed, there is the, Mongoloid spot', a deeply pigmented patch commonly present in the secral region which generally disappears soon after birth. In recent years the non-visible characteristics of different racial groups, such as blood groups, mouth swabs, immune reactions and enzyme structures have increasingly been studied. The gene therapy is getting approvable in the modern day science. With the help of this we would know the migration history of people. One most recent major movement in 1253 on Kublai Khan's conquest of Yun-nan (China) hastened a final wave of Tai-speaking into Burma (Myanmar) and northern Indo-China. A small number of them entered in the northeast region of India, and mixed with varied population of diverse ethnic groups. Most of them held in reverence to Buddha or Bodhisattva in their localised form. But all are substantially the same. Sakyamuni's preaching carried by saffron-robbed monks walking all over.

The Scythians (Sakyans) had have been pushing out from their original homeland Central Asia from pre-historic times and Buddhism has been their religion, cult and philosophy. We need to have a systematic analysis and study at all levels to know their geneological link of Sakyans in the South-East Asia.

A new light has been thrown with the discovery of a large number of sculptures recently in China.

In 1996, some 400 Buddhist stone sculptures were discovered in eastern China at the Lonxing temple site in Qingzhau, Shandong province. One of the most significant archaeological findings of recent years, the discovery of these sculptures is of immense importance to the history of Buddhism in China. The Royal Academy of Arts, London has been exhibiting it for the first time, to see, 35 of these magnificent Buddhist treasures, under the caption return of Buddha. This is highlighting the influence of Buddhism and its culture, the code of action that Buddha taught could free mankind from suffering and egotism.

In sculpture Buddha is depicted in lotus posture (sitting cross leg) or standing on lotus flowers, embleming of purity (Bodhisattva).

There are generally certain Buddhist terminology which seems confusing, because it rooted from native languages, like Phra means Buddha in Burmese. Similarly, Arya means noble and a personification of Nirvana is called Arya Tara, who is identified with Sakti or the female principle (Manjusri). So, Buddhist terminology (words) have no precise equivalent in English. A few examples are given below:

Irridhi: Religious term and there is no genetic terms for such English words.

Sunnya: Religious term and no English equivalent

word. The near English meaning void, empty.

Samata: Religious word, equanimity.

Prasada: A gift from god. It makes another meaning clarity (awakening of faith, sudden awakening).

Vidya: Energy.

Karma: (a) Nyaya (Result of action being to himself in life).

(b) Samukya (Result of action later what survives physical death is said to be left over, Karma, Samsara).

Adhisthan: Determination.

Mutta: Love.

Matreya: Loving kindness of peace and happiness.

Tantra: Creative imagination (mystic Buddhism).

Vajra: Diamond.

Yana: Vehicle (Vajrayana=Diamond vehicle, high state of purity).

Janā: Gyana (skt), knowledge. Jana Marga (Saving knowledge of 4 entities).

Jhāna: Absorption Dhyana (skt), Meditation. In Japan developed a Zen, the form in which it is most widely known in the west today. In Chinese the word is 'Chan'. In India it is called Vipasana.

Kyaung: Buddhist monastery (a Burmese word).

Kyaung thaga: Attended in the monastery.

Avolokiteshvara: Goddess of merry, Bodhisattva. In Japan it is called Guanyin (Kannon, Kuan-Yin). It is most popular figure in Chinese Pure land devotionalism. Traditionally, Avoloitesvora was male and Tibetan Buddhism he acquired a female consort called white Tara. It has a thousand eyes and a thousand hands to see and help those distress.

Amitava: Infinite light, which is termed Amida in China and Japan, emanated in the form, the forefingers of each hand touching the thumb, thus forming two within the oval of the hands. The right hand circle represents the divine law of Buddha, the left circle, the human law of Buddha, the larger circle made by both hands experiencing the unity of the two.

According to Buddhist philosophy there are two schools of Buddhism—(one) Therovada (Hinayana): individual attainment the fruits of holi life Arahat, by destroying by sensual craving and ill will through mental power and (two) Mahayana (Bodhisattva) for benefiting all living creatures. One can accumulate merit by performing virtuous acts like donating in the temple or being generous to the monks and also financing religious festivals.

Nagarjuna about 56 B C founded Madhyamaka the attainment of Bodhisattva or the condition of a future Buddha with a view to save all living creatures in ages to come.

Apportion of it, is called Prasangika, faith in Amida Buddha. They look forward to rebirth in the pure land and the attainment of Nirvana in that land. It is called Jodo, Jade in Japan. The other form is called Zen believing to attain enlightenment in this life itself (Sarvastavadin). Besides, Prasangika there is another form called Svatantrika which is being followed in Tibet, Mongolia and Nepal. The central philosophy of Buddhism; the sole concern of Madhyamaka, advayavada is the purification of the faculty of knowing. Changes, purification comes through the training of mind Advaya means method of science of knowing. Yogochara school of mind originally began by Nagarjuna, later Asanga (310-

390), Vasubandhu (320-400) developed this school. Yogochara system went from Gandhara, East Afghanistan. The Chinese brought under their protection the silk route (Afghanistan-Iran-China and also Greece), the oasis towns from the attacks of Huns and Turks and Buddhism followed this route which soon carried all through Asia.

Buddhism is not orthodoxy and not afraid of god, non-soul, advaita (no unified subject) i.e., Sunyata. Buddha said world is void. In Madhyamaka the mind has to attain the unconditioned, the characteristic of Buddhism, Hinduism believe in Brahma, supreme God, the divine reality of which the entire universe is only a manifestation. Every soul is identical with the one, the universal soul (advaita-vedanta).

Buddhism believe in saving up 'paramis' (goodness) from one life to another. Those who have unique paramis accumulation they get enlightenment easily or at least less suffering (dukkha) in life. Their philosophy in life is serenity, the past existences of Sakyamuni is conjectural base on folklore of Jataka stories.

King Bhimbisar of Magadha was the main patron of Buddha and many ethnic tribes originated from therewith Buddhist cultural infusion. At that time many joined Buddha's Sangha (monastic life) wearing yellow garb (chibar) which is still iso-practice for a shorter duration, a must for those who believe from Sakyan clone.

One such ethnic tribal group are called 'Chakmas' the earliest inhabitants of Chittagong hill tracts on the eastern most edge of the Himalayan ranges meeting with the Bay of Bengal in Bangladesh. These is no sufficient historical record of their origin. Some historian suggest they are from Champa (north Bihar which was a strong hold of Buddhist centre of

7-8th centuries). In the opinion of others they are from east (Burma). The probable explanation of the origin of Chakma might be: Chew (Champa) + Ma (people), like the writing Shan in English, written as Scian in France. They are best known for their steadfastness in Buddhist faith from very ancient time. The word Chakma can also be spelt as Tsakma–Burmese (T is pronounced as ch in English). They were 10 (ten) varieties when they were on the basin of Tsangpho (Brahmaputra)–these were:

1. Phwa-ho	2. Tai-yo	3. Ang-ngu
4. Bor-ua	5. Bung-ngu	6. Zotia
7. Bur-se-ke	8. Undu	9. Talao
10. Ang-ngu		

In the space of time their variety (clan) increased to over 30 (thirty) within it, after having inhabitant of the Chittagong hill tracts, about the Arakan hills. No Chakma ever has difficulty in understanding languages of Indian union originating from Indo-Aryan.

They are the aggrieved Tribal Buddhist, as when the world intellectuals were in the spree on making 'Hydro Electric Dams', for creating human comforts, Chakmas of CHT became the victims of it, some 50 years back, and still at the receiving end. Their suffering began to unfold, which has been described by Madam Adam Curle, London, which reads as follows:

From 1956 to 1959, I was an adviser to the Pakistan Planning Commission my responsibilities spread to East Pakistan, which is (now Bangladesh) and included the remote area beyond the Bay of Bengal, which was the homeland of the Chakmas, the largest of several tribal groups in the Chittagong Hill Tracts. One of my main responsibilities was to look into particular problems. Such as tribal conflict, famines, epidemics and so on.

Early in 1957, there were rumours in Karachi (then

the federal capital of Pakistan where the planning was located) that a dam was to be built in the CHT, which might flood out a few hundred tribal people living in the steep valleys behind the dam. But nobody knew much more. A couple of colleagues and I decided to go and assess the Chief town of the CHT by jeep, and after that further travel was also by elephant, country boat, or foot through beautiful wooded hills and steep valleys.

The local people knew something alarming was in the air, but were not sure what. They told us they said they had seen men painting lines on trees, but did not know what they signified. I was captivated by the Chakmas. Rangamati and the area upstream from the town predominantly populated by those delightful Buddhist people. They were artistic, cheerful, and hospitable. They lived in houses perched on top of stilts which, if over crowded tended to sway. Wherever we went we were offered hospitality. On one occasion when a large group had come to visit and drink rice wine, the sway was too much for the stilts and the whole structure sank gently to the ground. We felt, in a silly western way, guilty for this, but the Chakmas laughed and said was an old house and was bound to collapse soon anyway.

Children played in the bright waters of innumerable streams. Old men pottered round with hose. The valley were fertile and it seemed no one was undernourished or hungry. Beautiful girls wave the cloths which they something covered their breasts. For several days travelled with the uncle of the young head of the Chakma nation, the Chakma Rai. The situation gradually became clearer. Yes, the dam was going to be built, indeed was already being built, as we saw with our own eyes on the journey back – a great gash through the forest, hundreds of men's shifting buckets of soil, a hosted for the foreign engineers where feeling like traitors, we were given eggs and sausages for breakfast.

The dam would be completed. No doubt of that, powerful American firms had already spent millions on it. The backed up water would flood the fertile valleys. What then? The people would be displaced–driven up into the inhospitable hills or to the alien and non-Buddhist coastal areas. This gentle and creative civilization would disappear. In the last phase of our journey, the unhappy face of the future became increasingly clear to us and our Chakma friends. It was miserably sad. And justifiably for the nightmares soon become the reality. Ironically, too for in most respects the dam was failure, particularly as a generator of energy.

I returned to Karachi and did what I could, but the dam construction could not be reversed. We persuaded the government to set up an organization to mitigate the hardships that the Chakmas would inevitably suffer. There were scheme to develop agriculture round the shores of the lake, to populated it with fishes, and to build up a fishing industry. Experts on terracing were brought in from Indonesia to show how the hitherto wild hillside could be cultivated to replace (partially) the valleys. There were plans to educated young Chakmas in skills appropriate to their changed of fulfillment history saw to that.

In 1971, the Bengali people of East Pakistan protested against the tyranny of the drunken Pakistan President Yahya Khan. He once unleashed a vicious campaign of almost genocidal repression. India then intervened and the Pakistan army a thousand miles from us base could only surrender. Thus, Bangladesh was born. But history is replete with examples of how people, freed from oppression themselves, proceed to subjugate and repress minority groups with in their own border. The new order of Bangladesh had no sympathy with the harmless Buddhist people of the CHT. It cast envious eyes on the territory of this negligible minority and encouraged the increasingly violent incursion of settlers, most of whom would stick at nothing to establish themselves in this delightful country and have only contempt for its age long inhabitants. A few of these remain, but as a whole the Chakmas are a sadly damaged and scattered people."

(1. Discoveries in China)

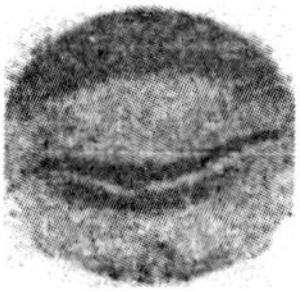

RETURN OF THE BUDDHA: THE QUINGZHOU DISCOVERIES

Opening the Buddha's eyes

Buddha became the central symbol of Buddhism, serving as a focus for meditation, devotion or ritual and as an expression of peace, harmony and the power of enlightenment. The majority of the sculptures in the exhibition represent Buddhas. Buddhist figures are rendered as ageless, passionless and flawless beings, their expressions introspective and compassionate. The treachings of the Buddha are extremely complex but in essence concentrate on finding a way to end suffering by overcoming the green and ignorance that cause it. The road to this goal is based on self-discipline and knowledge.

The Buddha's near-absence of specific attributes and ***individualising features indicates his unworldliness.*** *The utter simplicity of his appearance is coupled with a sophisticated gestural language. Such symbolic hand gestures, or 'mudras', effectively convey powerful messages to the devout beholder. For instance,* the hand held upright with palm facing outwards, the 'abhaya mudra', represents the gesture of protection and means 'Have no fear', while the palm pointing downwards in the 'varada mudra' indicates 'Your wish is granted'.

According to tradition, thirty-two unusual physical characteristics were ascribed to the Buddha, including the 'ushnisha', or protruberance on his head, which represents trancendental knowledge and wisdom. Other features include sapphire blue hair and golden skin, long and elegant curving eyebrows, crystal clear eyes with long eyelashes and a long straight nose. His elongated earlobes are a sign of Sakyamuni's renunciation of the world and an allusion to the elaborate earrings he would have worn as a prince before surrendering his worldly life to seek enlightenment.

A Buddhist statue was not complete until the eyes were painted. The 'eye opening ceremony' was a major ritual in creating a Buddha sculpture, transforming a piece of wood or stone carved with the Buddha's form into a sacred figure. It was carried out with great public ceremony. By lifting the figure onto another level of existence, worshippers could then offer the Buddha their prayers as well as asking for his help and intercession.

Among the sculptures found at Quingzhou are a number of extremely rare figures which relate to the concept of 'dharma', a system of duties and values. These Buddhist teachings are represented on one of the sculptures included in the exhibition which is covered in a relief showing a series of scenes. The carvings aren't detailed enough to allow an exact interpretation

Bodhisattvas

Bodhisattvas are beings who renounce nirvana in order to help others achieve enlightenment. Acting as intercessors they guide others towards understanding and release from the cycle of life, death and rebirth. In figural triads bodhisattvas stand in attendance on either side of the Buddha.

Though the bodhisattvas share many of Buddha's distinctive features, such as the 'ushnisha', or cranial protruberance, their appearance is often more worldly. Rather than wearing a monastic robe like the Buddha, bodhisattvas often wear princely attire, including jewellery.

Although bodhisattvas are enlightened beings who have attained liberation from the remorseless round of rebirth, they voluntarily postpone their own entry into nirvana in order to help all forms of sentient beings attain this supreme release. Their lavish jewellery indicates their connection to the living world.

One of the bodhisattvas shown here is adorned with body chains, bands of pearls, neckbands – still with traces of gilding on them – necklaces, ornamental clasps and other jewellery. The heavy body chain of pearls is interspersed with connecting elements of coral and metal. His head too is crowned with a ribbon of pearls and embellished with other decorative features such as lotus blossoms.

In addition to crowns and necklaces, great emphasis was placed on the decorative carving of such details as hair. Long ribbons often bind the bodhisattvas' hair, streamers fall from their object. The complex and finely worked pendants that appear on images of bodhisattvas found at Qingzhou are rarely seen in sculpture from neighbouring regions.

The model for the sumptuous and costly jewels decorating these figures was drawn from the images of noble Indian families. However, the bodhisattvas' jewellery didn't just represent earthly riches, it was also a metaphorical expression of the spiritual riches of their enlightened state.

Triads

The largest of the Longxing temple statues include a number of figural triads, of which the most impressive is over three metres tall. This triad weighs about one tonne, though its maximum thickness is only 35 cm. Its surprisingly slender structure is probably the reason it broke into several pieces at an early date. Besides the missing fragments, there is evidence of some early repair work.

The overall structure is complex. In the lower part stands the main figure of the Buddha flanked by two bodhisattvas. The figures, carved in relief, are cut out of a background, which takes the form of an almond shaped mandorla, symbolizing the sacred aura that radiates around the Buddha. The bodhisattvas stand on lotus flowers, emblems of purity.

The central Buddha figure is larger than the bodhisattvas and constitutes the most prominent element. He stands on a base that narrows into the tenon, resembling a leaf stalk, which would have anchored the sculpture into a base. Between the figures, exquisitely carved flying dragons – ancient mystical and invincible creatures – coil down to the base of the lotuses.

The detail of the carving is such that the dragons' eyes, teeth, scales and claws are clearly visible, while their elegantly curved bodies and serpentine tails contrast starkly with the static figures beside them. The inclusion of characteristically Chinese dragons within the triad demonstrates how the ancient Chinese world-view became incorporated into Buddhist faith. In East Asia, these mythical creatures are thought of as bringers of good fortune and traditional blessings such as water and fertility. Water spouts from the dragons' mouths onto lotus blossoms bursting with buds and leaves. These motifs, which support the lotus buds, serve as platforms on which the attendants stand to form a symmetrical composition.

Crowning the mandorla, flame-like heavenly beings known as 'apsaras', carved in high relief, flicker and hover at its tip. Among them are musicians, dancers and donor figures. On some triads they support a flying shrine or 'stupa', used to contain the remains of the Buddha, while on others they offer gifts or hold instruments of various kinds. Their coloured mantles flutter behind them, like lively streamers, soaring upward as they dance or play music. 'Apsara' originate in Indian mythology, demonstrating once more the wide-ranging sources incorporated into the visual vocabulary of these sculptures.

Exhibition Programme 2002

Sackler Wing

RETURN OF THE BUDDHA

The Qingzhou Discoveries

Supported by the RA Exhibitions Patron Group

26 April — 14 July 2002

In 996, some 400 Buddhist stone sculptures were discovered in eastern China at the Longxing temple site in Qingzhou, Shandong Province. One of the most significant archaeological findings of recent years, the discovery of these sculptures is of immense importance to the history of Buddhism in China. Since they were unearthed, the sculptures have been pieced together, cleaned and conserved. This exhibition will be the first opportunity in this country to see 35 of these magnificent treasures. Buried for almost one thousand years, following suppressions of Buddhism during the reign of Emperor Huizong (1119 AD), the statues to be displayed at the Royal Academy data from 386-577 AD. The display of these limestone sculptures of Buddhas and their attendant Bodhisattvas, will reveal the outstanding refinement of the carving. The sculptures, beautifully formed faces are lifelike, with ageless, delicate features. Many bear the remains of the original blue, green and ochre paint; some also retain the gold applied to the body of the Buddha to reflect his enlightened state.

Main Galleries

SUMMER EXHIBITION 2002

11 June—19 August

Sponsored by A.T. Kearney

The Royal Academy's annual exhibition, bringing together paintings, sculptures, drawings and models by many of Britain's most distinguished artists and architects, is the world's largest open contemporary art exhibition. The majority of works are for sale and prizes totalling £50,000 are offered to artists in various categories. Following Peter Blake's innovative hand of the Summer Exhibition 2001, leading sculptor Bryan Kneale RA, takes over as Senior Hanger for 2002.

RA Schools

RA SCHOOLS SHOW

13 June—24 June 2002

Sponsored by Debenhams Retail plc

Highlighting the work of final-year students who have successfully completed the only three-year postgraduate course in painting and sculpture in the country.

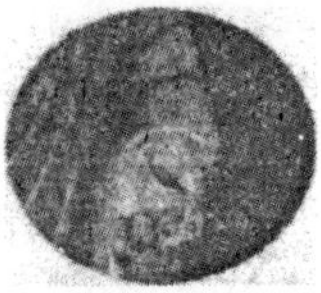

26 April—14 July

Supported by the RA Exhibition Patrons Group

In 1996 a startling discovery was made in Shandang province eastern China. Warkmen engaged in clearing land for a school sports field in the town of Qingzhou unearthed a hoard of more than 40 Buddhist sculptures. The quality and number of the sculptures made this one of the most intriguing and significant archaeological excavations of recent years.

According to early written sources the area in which the sculptures made found once formed part of Longxing Temple, a name that means 'Dragon Spring'. The discovery presents us with a challenging question: why were so many figures of Buddha buried at some point in the twelfth century in a carefully constructed pit within the precincts of a monastery?

A number of theories have been proposed. The statues show evidence of damage and repair. They may have fallen victim to Buddhist suppressions in the name of Daoism. Or, they might be the survivors of previous suppressions, collected and interred as part of a deliberate ritual ceremony. Whatever the reason, the discovery of a Buddhist treasury at the former temple site confirms the important role that Longxing played as a centre of Buddhist culture in the Qingzhou region during the sixth century.

Since then, the sculptures have been pieced together, cleaned and conserved. Thirty-five of the best-presented figures — all carved from limestone and created within a fifty-year period — have been selected for this exhibition. Among the statues uncovered are exquisite examples of Buddhas, bodhisattvas (attendants of the Buddha) and triads, in which a Buddha, flanked by two bodhisattvas, stands against a leaf-shaped nimbus.

The majority of the pieces date from the period of the Northern dynasties and in particular to the Northern Qi period (550–577). The figures show the sculptural styles that developed as Buddhism spread along the trade routes across Central Asia, mixing foreign with Chinese qualities. Stylistically, the sculptures can be divided into two groups, with earlier pieces retaining characteristically Chinese features such as elaborately carved dragons, while later figures have the grace and voluptuousness often associated with the Indian Subcontinent.

This exhibition marks the first presentation in Europe of a whole artistic tradition largely unknown to western audiences. Return of the Buddha will provide the first — and last — opportunity to see this significant group of Chinese Buddhist sculptures before they return to the new Qingzhou Municipal Museum.

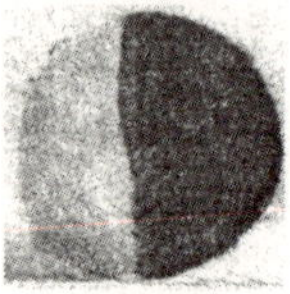

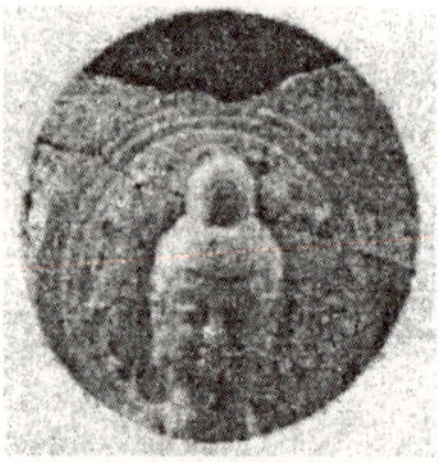

The origins of Buddhism can be traced back to the life of the Indian prince Siddhartha Gautama (c. 563–483 BC). He came to be known as Sakyamuni 'Sage of the Sakya clan', after he renounced his aristocratic roots and life of

luxury and set off on a path to find the cause of suffering. After years of asceticism and meditation, Sakyamuni attained enlightenment, whereupon he was called the Buddha, the 'Enlightened One.'

Sakyamuni devised a code of action that he believed could free humankind from suffering and egotism. That code is embodied in the central doctrine of Buddhism: the Four Noble Truths and the Eightfold Path. Following this doctrine can lead to 'nirvana' or release from the cycle of life, death and rebirth. Shakyamuni, known as the historical Buddha, is just one manifestation of enlightenment, which includes other Buddhas in past and future realms.

Buddhism spread from north-east India to many parts of Asia, reaching China by the first century AD. At first, the land of Daosim and Confucianism resisted these foreign teachings. However, the strong support given to Buddhism by emperors of the Wei dynasties eased its acceptance and ensured that the religion established itself. The Northern Wei, originally a nomadic people, conquered China in 386 and rapidly adopted Chinese customs. Their assimilation of indigenous Chinese traditions had direct repercussions on Buddhist art.

For a long time Chinese Buddhist sculpture had taken its lead from Indian religious artwork. However, by the end of the fifth century, Buddha figures were no longer shown in their Indian clothes, but wearing traditional Chinese robes.

In around 550 this development in favour of Chinese imagery was curtailed by a change of dynasties when the Northern Qi — led by non-Chinese — came to power and began to re-introduce foreign practices.

The influence of Indian Buddhist models clearly played a major role in the art created under the Northern Qi (550—557), breaking with the stylistic conventions of the earlier period. Indeed, Indian Buddhist monks were welcome in the areas under the dynasty's control. The Buddha figures of the Northern Qi period, distinguished by a greater naturalism, tend to the carved in the round and clad in thin robes, which cling to the body. The completely new style of Buddhist image avoided decorative carving and instead revealed the undulating contours of the body.

The Return of the Buddha

The Qingzhou Discoveries

26 April# 151; 14 July 2002

Supported by the RA Exhibition Patrons Group

In 1996 an extraordinary treasury of some 400 Chinese stone sculptures of the Buddha was discovered in eastern China at the Longxing temple site in Qingzhou, Shandong Province. Buried for over 900 years, the discovery of these sculptures is one of the most fascinating and significant archaeological finds of recent years. The hoard offers remarkable insights into the nature and tradition of Chinese Buddhist art and is immensely important for the history of Buddhism. 35 sculptures will be on show at the RA, providing the first opportunity in this country to see the finest possible examples of a whole artistic tradition that has long been invisible to Western audiences.

The high quality of the sculptures and the vast number pose intriguing questions. Why were so many Buddhist figures dating primarily to the sixth century buried in a carefully constructed pit within the precincts of a monastery? From the Western Han period (206 BC to AD 220) to the beginning of the Ming (AD 1368), Qingzhou was the political and economic capital of Shandong Province and important centre of Buddhist culture. Though Buddhist suppressions during this time caused the destruction of monasteries and objects of worship, it is unlikely that anti-Buddhist fervour alone was responsible for the burial of the sculptures. The evidence suggests that they were interred deliberately as part of a ritual.

The Longxing monastery has long disappeared and the site is now home to the Shefan primary school. In October 1996, construction workers levelling the sports field discovered a shallow pit, 60 metres square and three metres deep, filled with broken Buddhist sculptures. Within ten days, all the fragments were removed. Since then, the sculptures have been pieced together, cleaned and conserved. Among the statues uncovered were equisite examples of Buddhas and Bodhisattvas (attendants of the Buddha) and triads, in which a Buddha flanked by two Bodhisattvas, stands against a magnificent almond-shaped mandorla. Many sculptures still bear the original blue, red, green and orchre paint and a number of the statues also retain the gold applied to the face and body of the Buddha to indicate his sun-like radiance.

Carved from limestone, the sculptures on display all date from the period of the Northern dynasties and in particular to the Northern Qi period (550-577). The figures show the sculptural styles that developed as Buddhism spread along the trade route across Central Asia mixing foreign with Chinese qualities Stylistically they are divided into two groups, with earlier pieces retaining characteristically Chinese features such as elaborately carved dragons, while later figures bear the grace and voluptuousness often associated with the Indian Sub-continent. The delicate features and introspective expressions of these lifelike Buddhist sculptures brilliantly evoke the dignity of their inherent compassion and sense of enlightenment.

The Royal Academy of Arts' renowned exhibitions of non-western art include the landmark exhibition Africa: Art of a Continent (1995). Future presentations include Aztecs (16 November 2002 - 11 April 2003) and The Adventures of Hamza, an exhibition of the Hamzanama, a 16th Century Mughal Manuscript (Spring 2003).

Organistion

The exhibition has been organised by the Royal Academy of Arts and the State Administration of Cultural Heritage, People's Republic of China. It has been selected by Albert Lutz, Director of the Museum Rietberg, Zurich, and Edmund Capon, Director of the Art Gallery of New South Wales, Sydney, with Norman Rosenthal, Exhibitions Secretary, Royal Academy of Arts and Giuseppe Eskenazi. Cecilia Treves, Exhibition Curator, RA, has collaborated on the presentation of the exhibition.

Tour Dates

Return of the Buddha is a touring exhibition. It was shown at the Altes Museum, Berlin (20 September - 18 November 2001) and is currently on show at the Museum Rietberg, Zürich (13 January - 7 April 2002). It will be presented at the RA as its third and final European venue.

Supporters

Generous support for this exhibition has come from the RA Exhibition Patrons Group, Mrs. Arthur M. Sackler and two anonymous benefactors. The Royal Academy receives no public subsidy and is entirely reliant on self-generated income and charitable donations. Exhibition Patrons are dedicated individuals who appreciate the Royal Academy's exhibition programme and invest in its continuing success by making an annual tax- effective donation. They are encouraged to become directly involved in the artistic life of the Academy and gain a unique insight into the creative process through which each exhibition evolves.

Catalogue

RA Publications is producing a comprehensive catalogue to accompany the exhibition. Fully illustrated with colour photographs, the catalogue features an introduction by Dr Albert Lutz, Director of the Museum Rietberg, Zurich, and essays by leading scholars, exploring new insights in Chinese Buddhist art and examining its iconography, style, materials and techniques.

Audioguide

Following the success last year of the free audioguide for Botticelli's Dante: The Drawings for The Divine Comedy, the Royal Academy has again included the exhibition audioguide in the admission price. The audioguide, produced by Antenna Audio, provides a comprehensive guide to the exhibition, enabling visitors to fully appreciate the historic importance of these sculptures.

Dates and Opening Hours

Press View: Tuesday 23 April 2002, 10 am – 2 pm

Private Views: Wednesday 24 and Thursday 25 April 2001. Open to public: Friday 26 April to Sunday 14 July 2002. 10 am – 6 pm daily (last admission 5.30 pm). Late night opening: Fridays until 10 pm (last admission 9.30 pm).

Admission

£7.50 full charges; £6.50 concessions; £5.50 full-time students; £3 12-18 years + income support; £2 8-11 years. Admission includes exhibition audioguide.

Tickets

Tickets are available daily at the RA. For advance bookings, call Way Ahead on tel: 0870 830 0201 or visit www.wayahead.com

For further press information, please contact Caroline Birchall or Sarah Davies at the RA Press Office on tel: 0207 300 5615/5610, fax: 0207 300 5886 or email: press.office@royalacademy.org.uk

For public information, please print tel: 020 7300 8000 and www.royalacademy.org.uk

Sackler Wing

Masters of Colour: Derain to Kandinsky

80 Masterpieces from The Merzbacher Collection

27 July – 17 November 2002

This exhibition will show some 70 paintings and sculptures from the exceptional collection of Werner and Gabrielle Merzbacher. Over more than 30 years the Merzbachers, of Switzerland, have assembled one of Europe's greatest private collections. It celebrates the expressive, decorative and constructive uses of colour during the late 19th and early 20th centuries. Featuring works by many of the modern masters, the exhibition will include paintings by Matisse, Picasso, Braque, Kandinsky and Klee, and sculptures by Modigliani and Calder. This uniqe collection, which features masterpieces from Impressionism, Fauvism, German Expressionism, and the Russian Avant-garde, has been regularly drawn on by museums and galleries worldwide. Previously exhibited as a collection only in Israel and Japan, this will be the only opportunity in Europe to view these works together.

Main Galleries

Aztecs

16 November 2002-11 April 2003

The Royal Academy will be hosting a ground-breaking exhibition devoted to the cultural riches of Mexico's Aztec past. This five-month long show will highlight the splendours, variety and sophistication of Aztec civilisation. One of the most ambitious exhibitions ever staged at the RA, it will bring together a large number of works never previously shown outside Mexico to make the most comprehensive survey of Aztec culture ever mounted. The exhibition will start by examining the origins of the Aztecs. The main part of the exhibition will be devoted to the art of the Aztec Empire itself from 1325 to its demise in 1521, with the largest gallery dedicated to a dramatic display centred around the Great Temple of Tenochtitlan, present day Mexico City. It will also explore the long-term resonance of Aztec art and culture and will show how, following the arrival of the Spanish in 1519, the foundations of modern-day Mexico were laid. In addition to monumental sculptures in stone, wooden objects and ceramics, the exhibition will reunite several of the most important pictorial manuscripts or codices. It will also include spectacular works of art made of turquoise mosaics, gold and other precious materials, of which only a small number have survived - these are among the most exquisite objects ever made in the ancient Americas.

Library Print Room Displays*

Julian Trevelyan RA and his Circle: Prints and Drawings
28 May–early October 2002

Friends Room Exhibitions**

Norman Adams RA
12 April–20 June 2002

New English Art Club

21 June–11 September 2002

**The Library Print Room is open to the public : Tuesday to Friday, 11 am to 1 pm and 2 pm to 4 pm.*

***The RA Friends Room is open to the public from 4 pm to 6 pm daily.*

For further press information, please contact Caroline Atkinson or Sarah Davies on tel: 020 7300 5615/5610, fax: 020 7300 5886 or email press.office@royalacademy.org.uk

For public information, please telephone 020 7300 8000.

Raja Tridiv Roy, they simply belong

2. The Shrine on the Hill

Alikadam, in the south of Hill Tracts, was one of the ancient capitals of the Chakma Kings. There are still vestiges of ruined palaces, temples and ponds. An occasional coin of those bygone days still forms a part of a young girl's necklace. A hill is even today known as Pagla Mura, after the "Pagla Raja" Shatua. Near the confluence of the Matamuri and the Toin there once stood a shrine on the hill—surrounded by a cluster of champa trees. It is said that on certain nights a blue luminescence could be discerned around the shrine which, however, vanished at human approach; but not the lingering fragrance of incense and sandalwood....

The King's favourite horse was a chestnut bay that was not born in the royal stables but under a champa tree. One day as Shatua, in his pre-dawn ride, cantered past the forest of champas he heard the pitiful neighing of a horse in pain. The King, ever sensitive to the sufferings of others, turned back, dismounted and raced up the knoll. And there he discovered the new born foal which he named Champa....

Champa is dead. The King has not he heart to ride another horse. It is not yet dawn. He saunters out of the palace gates and ambles about dispiritedly. An unseen force seems to draw him toward the cluster on the hill where years ago Champa first stood on shaky, new found, legs.

In the faint morning light he perceives, under the self-same tree, a monk in yellow robes meditating in the lotus posture. He appears to be in a trance, his body rigid, his eyes fixed, unblinking. Shatua, sensing that intrusion would be unwelcome, retires behind a tree and observes the mendicant in enthralled silence.

Presently, a blue green glow seems to emanate from the monk and still in the same posture, he is elevated gently as though by some invisible hand. The sitting figure floats about, then remains immobile, suspended in mid air, his unseeing eyes still riveted on the tip of his nose.

The monk gradually floats down to earth. The glow grows faint, then vanishes. The rigidity is gone and he seems to breathe. His eyelids stir and he blinks. He is normal again, a man sitting under a tree, relaxed, serene.

Shatua had heard of Yogis and Tantrics but had ever been skeptical of their prowess in the occult, dismissing most of the accounts as exaggerated hearsay. Now he is astounded at seeing a man actually levitate before his every eyes. He goes forward and bows.

"Holy One, I am amazed at what I have witnessed. Are you an Arahat?"

"No, son, still a seeker."

"Do you follow the esoteric doctrine handed down through Kasyapa the elder?"

"The Guru did not specify. He said the Tathagata showed the way."

"Holy one, if I become your chela will you teach me levitation and the power to read minds and look into past lives?"

The monk smiles. "An Ekachari does not accept chelas, son. He sojourns alone. He can merely give guidance to one who seeks. He has achieved Jatiswar knowledge and a little of levitation but cannot read minds — not all minds."

"Tell me, then, what must I do?"

"You must vow not to speak of the powers you may gain except only to him whom you may teach. And you may teach only to those with the capacity to learn."

"But how will I determine that?"

"You will be told. You must also vow never to use your powers for evil."

"I vow."

"To observe these conditions until death?"

"Yes, Holy One."

"Remember that mind controls matters and will controls mind. Learn to view all phenomena through knowledge, not through the senses. Consider the faculty of sight. Every impression—every image that the eye conveys to the brain in the inferior image—the image of limited truth. The mind must superimpose the true image, in all its perspectives, in its entirety. Now, a word about breathing...."

The King has had a shrine built on the knoll of champas. Unfailingly, ever Tuesday and Saturday he retires there and remains alone from midnight to sunrise. No one, on pain of death, is permitted within a radius of two hundred cubits of the shrine. There are whispers that the King undertakes strange activities there. Some say, he hangs head down like a bat, changes form, that he practices suspended animation.

One evening, at the palace, when the King has retired to his bed chamber, he heard a knock.

"Who is it?"

"My Lord, it is I."

Shatua opens the door to let in Amangali, his Chief Queen. Her mind has been poisoned by certain courtiers, whose insidious promptings insist that the King has entered into evil ways, and that only she can set things aright before it is too late. These Cassandras had predicted depletion of the royal coffers long ago, yet, despite the King's charitable exuberance the royal treasury is fuller than ever and the people more prosperous.

"My Lord, Why do you prevaricate? Is it evil—what you do in the shrine?"

"No, Amangali, there is no evil involved. I have told you so before. Why do you persist in this matter?"

"People speak of strange goings-on. And there is a great change in you. You do not delight in our company any longer. Is it a fancy for some new woman?"

Shatua laughs, "Women do not delight me any more, Amangali; nor I them, I dare say. I cannot feel any passion for them, for I see beyond the externals—I perceived the defilements they are composed of."

"Are we then repulsive to you—even the beautiful Damayanti, whose society you could not have enough of before this change in you?"

"No, they do not repulse me – it is that they do not attract me either."

"Damayanti is pining for you, though pride makes her hide her heart."

"And what makes you hide yours, Amangali?"

"I? But......my head.........I feel weak." She faints.

Shatua sighs. "Poor misguided woman. Yet what is fated has to be." He restores her, then goes to the chamber of Damayanti, his youngest wife. At his approach she rushes forward to greet him and then abruptly draws back recoiling at her own rebounding passion that could not penetrate the King's aura. She blinks back her tears, uncomprehending, hurt.

"Forgive me, Little One, I should have warned you. Believe me, I would speak, were it possible."

Damayanti looks at him through her tears. The King sits on a low stool by the window across the room.

"Do you still love me, Little One?"

Damayanti nods. "Yes, more than ever. But my Lord's love has dried up-like a marsh in summer heat."

The scent of jasmines wafts in through the open

window. Through a pause in the northern flight of clouds the full moon is visible again in its splenderous isolation. The king turns from the window and looks at her. There is a wistful smile in his eyes.

"It has not dried up, Little One, only changed form."

The plaintive note of a distant flute lends the night an added poignancy.

"Now, listen. My end is drawing near—a violent end."

"No, never. I shall not let it happen. Who dares hurt my noble king?"

"There is greed and hatred and delusion around us. The die has been cast. And my former Karma impels me toward such an end." He look at the Matamuri flowing on in its silent, incessant, continuity.

"I shall take form only once more, if you help."

"I?"

"Yes, Little One. I cannot rely on any one else. May I ask this favour of you? A difficult one, though."

She looks at her Lord and is stricken at the expression of infinite sadness and hope. "Anything, my heart, anything."

He sighs and turn to gaze at the moon-bathed Matamuri and ponders its illusion of permanency, of immutability. Yet it is in a state of perpetual flux, not a drop remaining in one spot for even a moment on its journey to the sea. But then what is river without its banks or a being without its Name and Form? Perhaps, its essential no-self, no longer a part of the Whole, but the Whole itself.

"After I am killed, before the rise of the seventh day sun you must cremate me, you with one trusted maid alone. Could you, would you, Little One? Then collect the ashes and release them where the Toin joins the Matamuri."

The Queen is speechless.

"It is either yes or no. I give you my word that what you do is to prevent the recurrence of evil, the evil in me, the last vestige of it."

The young Queen bites her lips to smother the swelling tears. "Yes, my lord, I shall do as you bid."

"Do you give your solemn word—no matter what I—or any one else says or does—that you shall do exactly as I have said?"

"I do."

"May all accumulated merits of my myriad existences surround you in blessing. Now, the time is nigh, I must go away. Grieve not, Little One, all things pass away. Remember evil can never be cured by evil but by love alone. This is an eternal verity."

It is past midnight. Amangali creeps out of the palaces gates and stealthily proceeds toward the shrine. She peers through the peephole she had had gouged out in the wall earlier. All is darkness within save for winking green-blue glow-worms—or so they appear to her. She watches spellbound. The King, in rapt concentration, is washing his heart and entrails. Amangali shrieks at the sight—again and again.

Shatua hastily completes his ritual ablutions and rushes out. But by then she has made good her escape. Some feel that the rude disturbance in the midst of such a psychically delicate operation deterred him from reinserting his vital organs properly. Others are of the view that he was then in some sort of suspended animation and his real psyche could not re-enter his body. The surmises are many. It is given out that the King's mental equilibrium is affected. And thenceforth he is known as the Mad King—the Pagla Raja.

People are immensely saddened at this tragic development and begin to murmur at the apathy in the palace, for no physicians or witch doctors are permitted to see the king. Some say that he is seized with deep melancholia and is confined to a room where he paces ceaselessly and mutters to himself. Some whisper that there is a conspiracy to murder the king and that in fact he is perfectly sane. One day this is what happens:

Knowing the king's pet avertion to elephants, someone raises an alarm that an elephant has gone berserk. Shatua thrusts out his head through the window to see for himself. Amangali's father severs it with a single blow of the axe. The head, however, does not fall on the ground. Unaccountably it vanishes. The conspirators quietly secret the body out of the palace and burry it near the shrine. They dare not announce the king's death for people would demand to see his body; and a headless one would not be acceptable, if for no other reason, as clear evidence of foulplay. As the king is childless Amangali takes the reign of government in her hands. People hear garbled accounts of the assassination and clamour for justice, and for a proper cremation. Amangali acquires the appellation, "Daughter of the Regicide."

But the head cannot be found, and this cannot be divulged. While public clamour mounts, Damayanti dreams. In her dream the king implores her to open his grave on the seventh day but not to cremate him, so that he may come back to life by his magic powers and avenge himself. The dream recurs again and again.

Before the dawn of the seventh day, Damayanti, accompanied by a maid, visits the grave which her trusted scouts had located earlier. They find the necessary implements, as instructed, then begin to dig. Damayanti finds the king whole, the severed head miraculously conjoined with the body, and the body warm with reviving life.

There is a tremendous struggle within her, a temptation to slink away and do nothing—and let the king come back to life and punish the perpetrators of this fulsome perfidy.

But again and again the king's voice and the infinite sadness and hope in his eyes comes back to mind—and her pledge—and his words:

"Evil can never be cured by evil but by love alone. This is an eternal verity."

She grits her teeth and with every fibre crying out against it, she yet carries out her king's last behest, and with her own hand ignitiies the incense strewn pyre of sandalwood.

The blushing eastern sky shyly awaits the appearance of her lord, the sun. Damayanti places the ashes in a ivory casket and wearily wends her way down to the confluence of the rivers. Tears coursing down her face, her heart breaking with anguish, she gently lowers the king's last remains into the river. Ever slowly, the casket sinks. The ripples widen in concentric circles, then vanish.

3

Ethnic Buddhism in Assam Valley

India's northeast region abuts to Myanmar and Tibet, where mighty Brahmaputra (in Tibet Tsangpho) river originates taking its westerly course throughout the state of Assam (Asom, Ayam).

Assam is in north-east India, nestling at the foothills of the Himalayas. It is known as the land of blue hills and red rivers. It is the melting spot of various Mongoloid races tribes, who came down from the Himalayas.

Assam is easily accessible from Myanmar (Burma) and Tibet as it has vast common geographical boundaries and contour of relationship through which many tribes swamped over Assam from ancient ages. The history corroborates that they all belong to Scythian, a number of tribes from Central Asia. They are the ethnic tribes of Assam of the present day; an off-shoot from the main line. Assam has been the gateway of India to south-east for trade, culture, civilization (Buddhism) from the earliest time. Therefore, migration became established from the dynastic Ahom Rule 1238 in Assam, who originates from Tais and Shans, known as Ahoms. History corroborates that Sakyan, Tais, Shans had assimiled before 500 B.C. It is clear in history Sakyan Kingdom at Tagaung (Burma) was dominated by Shans. The Sakyan King Binnakya Raja was overthrown and expelled by the invasion of tribes called Tarok and Tarok from Yun-nan (China), and the invaders were Tai or Shans. Subsequently they merged and assimilated together and became known as Myama.

This is the historical background of Ahoms originally Shan Tribes from upper Burma migrated to north-east Assam by crossing one Patkai hills and ruled over 600 years from 1228-1826 and there are many subgroups among them. Assam was in the hands of Burmese rule from 1819 to 1858 and East India Company from 1826 to 1858 A.D. Thereafter the administration of Assam along with India was in the hands of crown of England in 1858. This was the most violent trouble period in Assam and many returned back to Burma, but as the situation improved many got back to their earlier settlement in Assam. The colonial rulers made a survey of land in Assam. According to their survey, Assam, is ideal for growing tea. The river Brahmaputra as it emerges from the eastern Himalayas and flows west through Assam. The great rivers tributaries leaves scars of alluvial deposits in the lower slopes of the Mismi Hills. The Brahmaputra is known as the Dihang (Dihing) as it was cuts the high mountains and it course may be followed back through the deep hazefilled valleys, dispersed population in different circumstances in different areas of them—and yet a community. Assam tea has its distinction which originated in China. Assam is on the silk route India-China. Assam's Muga silk has a great distinction in the present day. This is how Assam has made its mark in the world map. Interestingly, it is also known for the last remnants of Buddhism in India. The Tai speaking communities are mainly of five sub-groups viz., Tai Khamtis, Tai Aiton, Tai Phakey, Tai Turung and Tai Khamyang. They are ardent Buddhist. Their Buddhist culture is very similar to Theravada lesser vehicle (Hinayan), which became dominant around 11th century in Myanmar. Their scriptures are in Pali language. Prior to the leviation of lesser vehicle (Hinayana), Greater Vehicle (Mahayana) was dominent in this region. There has been mingling which are as follows:

1. Fi – Suomung (deity protecting the village);
2. Fi – Dam (spirit of ancestors);
3. Fi – Nam (spirit of water);
4. Fi – Hung (spirit of tree);
5. Nang Khon Khaw (goddess of paddy).

They believe accumulating merit by performing virtuous acts like subsidizing a temple or being generous to monks and financing religious activities. They became inextricable in their Buddhist faith.

The next is Thai-Ahoms who ruled independent Assam, used to worship a deity 'Phura-Tara, (Phunatara), Phra-Lung meaning Buddha. Their Buddhist practices has greatly disappeared. They have formed a Phra-Lung council for the preservation their old ideology faith in Buddha. Similarly, their original language is now on the process of oblivion as they speak Assamese which is new Indo-Aryan language. But some of their rituals are identifying them clearly; one such ritual is called Chaklong or 'song-leng' (marriage custom), and the other the proposal of marriage is sent by adoring a bronze plate full of beetlenuts and gold coins covered with silk-towel printed with Tai art and paintings. There practices are enshrined in native traditions in Assam. Introduction of Riha-Mekhala: The Riha-Mekhala ensemble, especially the Riha was introduced into Assam by Ahoms and it is associated with other Tai races of Thailand and Indo-China. The other influx were from Tibet in successive waves in Assam and many offshoots from that great Mongolian family and many of them are regarded as first native settlers in Assam. They are ardent Buddhist of Mahayana traditions.

The great massive influx has taken place from west-north Bihar, Champa, Magadha and elsewhere. Assam was known Kamarupa at that time till the end of the Koch rule (17th century A D), and the ancient Kamarupa comprised the whole of north Bengal, including Koch Bihar and the Rangpur and Jalpaiguri district of Bengal. As one travels from western to eastern direction one will find clearly the cultural and physical differences of people, representing of the historical background of the area. The naming of people also differed like the Singpho tribe in Arunachal Pradesh is called Tsangpho in Tibet. Jingpho in China and Kochin in Myanmar. At Guwahati the capital of Assam, there are 5 (five) Buddhist monasteries, namely:

1. Narengi Temple, Therovada
2. Bamuni Maidan Temple, Therovada
3. Kharguli Temple, Therovada
4. Garchuk Temple, Therovada
5. Assam Temple, North Guwahati; Mahayana.

In every Tai village, in upper Assam there are Buddhist monasteries irrespective of population as for all their social activities turns around it.

In the first-half of the seventh century Chinese traveller Hiuen-Tsang visited Assam and made reference of Buddhism in his description. He did not mention which school of Buddhism was prevalent in Assam.

The Therovada Buddhist organisations are governed by (1) Assam Bhikkhu Sangha and the other (2) North-East Bhikkhu Sangha.

Life Animation Ceremony of Buddha Statue

The universe depends on air, earth, heat and water. The water (H_2O) is known widely by different forms depending on its calibration like ocean (sea), lake, river and convertable into streams by heat. Similarly the ice, snow, glacier, by cold. The frozening of water takes place at a very altitude from the sea level. So the living conditions where people have became accustomed to food habits that are grown there. The outside physical condition colour varies on the geographical conditions.

We are now coming on a new era to examine and explore if there is different kind of life in other planets and our connectivity with it. The present human race is now on in with this study, obsessed with this idea the human being is undergoing a rapid transformation in the present world – the highest order of transformation in the scientific era. This is the path of life knowing the unknown with hard work.

Science originates from zero (0) and it originated in India identifying divinity, purity (philosophically). Moksha the ultimate end to human existence to be realised through destruction.

There are mystic repetitions of the term 'Om' ! In Tibetan Buddhism and Hinduism, signifying beyond nothingness (Sunnya). It represents the elements as follows:

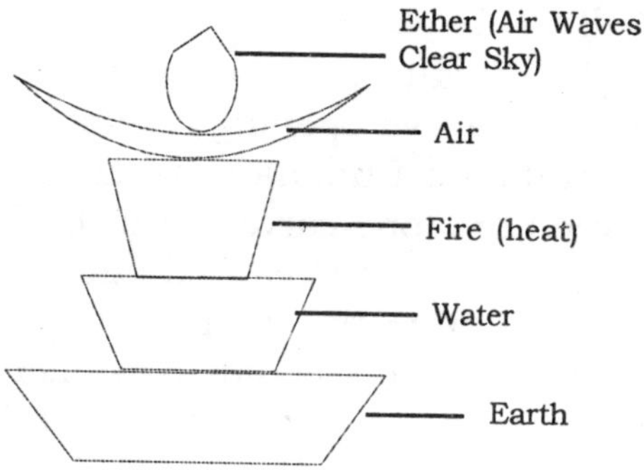

In the chemical science, over 100 different substances which have never been separated into chemical means and which alone or in combination constitute all matter; they are distinguished from each other by the number of electrons in their atoms outside the atomic nucleus.

The convergence of Buddhist and Hindu ideas emerged in India in northern Bihar around 700 A D. The idea of heaven comes from Hinduism. The tantra Tara (Shakti) added magico–religious sanctification. The Sanskrit term Avolokiteshvara means, the lord who looks down, a term suggestive Bodhisattva's loving care for humanity from the celestial height who uses a thousand eyes (understanding) and a thousand hands (actions) to see and help those in distress.

According to traditions, thirty-two unusual physical characteristics were ascribed to the Buddha, including the 'Ushnisha' or protruberance on his head, which represents transcendental knowledge and wisdom, other features include sapphire blue hair and golden skin, long and elegant curving eyebrows, crystal clear eyes with long eye lashes and a long straight nose. His elongated earlobes are a sign of Sakyamuni's renunciation of the world and an allusion to the elaborate earnings he would have worn as a prince before surrendering his worldly life to seek enlightenment.

A Buddhist statue was not complete until the eyes are painted. The 'eye opening ceremony' was a major ritual in creating a Buddha sculpture, transforming a piece of wood or stone carved with the Buddha's form into a sacred figure. It is carried out with great public ceremony. By lifting the figure onto another level of existence, worshippers could then offer the Buddha their prayers as well as asking for his help and intercession.

In the Therovada Buddhism this ceremony is called to bring alive the image of a Buddha. It is performed by a Bhikkhu Sangha (assembly more than five altogether). They would prepare the Buddha's statue well made by setting on candle lights and putting on sticks of smoothing fragrance. Then the monks (Therovada) would be holding out the seven articles (below) before the image of Buddha with chanting from 'Sutta Pitakas'.

1. Ghee (Indian Butter);
2. Long (Labanoja) (Syzygium Aromalicum);
3. Dalchini (Cinnamomum Tamala);
4. Elayachi (Eletteria Cardamomum);
5. Chandan (Santalum Album);
6. Jaiphal (Nutmeg Trolon Tiglium);
7. Trifala (a) Amla (gooseberg; emblica-officinalis) + (b) Haritaki (Termanalia Chebula) + (c) Bhibitaki (Termanalia Bellerica) a collective recitation.

Tara, Tantra (Shakti, Bodhisattva Manjusri)

It is the manifestation of the wisdom, compression, love and in particular the skillful activity of all enlightened beings. Buddhist Shakti is represented in Tara (female savior). The Buddha's Shakti was sometimes depicted as the goddess Prajna Paramita (Perfect Knowledge = Heart Sutra) like their Hindu counterparts Buddha and Bodhisattava were often depicted in sexual embrace with a Tara or Shakti. One meaning of this symbol is that world treats as opposite male/female, light/darkness, good/evil, Samsara /Nibbana – exist in a state of dynamic tension which the Tantra adept (Completely Skilled) must through superior knowledge, integrate. Interplay of Cosmic Sexuality (mysterism) i.e. Tantra without overcoming to an end. The emancipation of it is peace in awareness.

Tantric practitioners consider the peacock is a good symbol of their path, since it flourishes eating berries which other species find it poisonous.

In Samsara, to grow pearls there has to be some grit in Oyster Grit in dukkha, suffering.

Zen Tantra (Buddhist Psychology)

In Buddhism, there are three main approaches to self-training. First is the path of the renunciant. This person trains by changing the circumstances of their life quite radically. They cut-off all distractions and fill their life solely with experiences which reinforce commitment to the spiritual path. Buddha recommended that renunciants spend periods away from cities in the forest or mountains and adopt a simple lifestyle. On a lesser scale, we all know-how refreshing it can be to 'get away from it all' for a time. All Buddhists try to find at least some periods for retreat.

The second approach relies not so much upon changing our circumstances as on changing the way in which we act. This is the Bodhisattva path. A Bodhisattva is someone who feels the suffering of others. A Bodhisattva is active in the world. Bodhisattva trains by service to others. A modern Bodhisattva might be a therapist. The Bodhisattva sees the world through the eyes of others. Even if someone robs her, the Bodhisattva understands the need of the robber.

Finally, there is a third approach, called tantra. Tantra means to go directly to the 'pure land' by reconstructing every experience as a blessing. We ourselves thereby become divine beings 'through the practise of dharma we can come to change the way in which we experience things because, given that they have no ultimate reality in and of themselves, there is no reason for [negative] aspects of experience to dominate us.

Zen integrates all three approaches. It is firmly based on the renunciant tradition of early Buddhism. It has developed the Bodhisattva path in all its fullness and it incorporates the tantric (or *shingon*) method. Thus, an important Zen text is the Lotus Sutra chapter on Avalokita, Bodhisattva of compassion. According to the text, Avalokita appears in any form, anywhere, any time. This is basically a tantric text. The method it enjoys upon the practitioner is to regard every-thing that happens as a manifestation of Avalokita, which is to say, as an act of utmost compassion.

(b) Promoting Buddhist Network

It is recognised that there can be many interpretation of schools of Buddhism:

1. Theravada (Hinayana) Leser Vehicle - The objective to became Arahat, non-returners and no-suffering individual attainment. It is practised in India, Burma (Myanmar), Thailand.

2. Mahayana Greater Vehicle - For benefiting all living creatures. It exists in China, Korea, Vietnam, Cambodia and Japan.

3. Madhyamaka (Yogachara) the mind only - mainly attributing to Korea, Japan, China like Sato (Zen), Jodo or Jade faith in celestial Amida Buddha (lord of wisdom). Looking forward to rebirth in a pure land.

4. Svatantrika (Sautrantika) - It is mainly attributing to Tibet, Mongolia, Nepal and Bhutan. It branched off from the Sarvastivada some three hundred years after the Buddha's death.

A person who is interested to breathe freely has to learn 'Samatha' there is no equivalent word in English. It is known to be equanimity. In Buddhist terminology it is called 'Samadhi' (Visudhi Marga = purifying mind) leading to 'Jhana' (purity in wisdom/ insight knowledge-wisdom). One has to strive with diligence to gain undistracted of mind in 'Jhana' (eighteen chief kinds), namely:

(1) Contemplation of impermanence;
(2) Contemplation of suffering;
(3) Contemplation of not self;
(4) Contemplation of aversion;
(5) Contemplation of detachment;
(6) Contemplation of extinction;
(7) Contemplation of abandoning;
(8) Contemplation of waning;
(9) Contemplation of vanishing;
(10) Contemplation of change;
(11) Contemplation of the unconditioned;
(12) Contemplation of desirelessness;
(13) Contemplation of emptyness;
(14) Contemplation of insight into phenomena which is higher wisdom;
(15) Knowledge and vision according to reality;
(16) Contemplation of misery;
(17) Reflecting contemplation;
(18) Contemplation of luming away.

Insight wisdom means considering the nature of mind and matter, as mind and matter itself and not as father, mother or any other being; just as we peel the bark of a banna tree and thus make our wisdom into number of sections.

To purify one's mind by meditating on the Buddha which would require the power of concentration and by developing concentration one would be able to retain mind on one subject for a long time, leading purify to wisdom.

A Sketch of Self Awareness
by Dave C. Haris. 99. London.

1. William Robinson

A Descriptive Account of Assam. The name Assam is generally supposed to be derived from the Sanskrit term 'asama' a compound word formed from the negative particle, (a) and (Sam), equal signifying unequalled or unrivalled; but it seems probable that this derivation was merely an invention of the Brahmins, after the conversion of the last dynasty to the Brahminical faith. This dynasty was a tribal of Shyans (Shan), called Ahoms or Asom, who invaded the country, and from whom it might with greater probability have derived its present appellation.

Whilst the Kuch (Cooch) Rajas were possessing themselves of lower Assam, the Ahoms had invaded the south-eastern extremity of the valley; and their conquests, together with the settlements of the colonists of this race, led to the permanent distinction of Kamrup from Assam or lower from upper Assam.

2. Sir J.G. Scott

Burma from the earliest time to the present day p.6 Ahoms (Tai-Shan race)

Consequently they divided themselves into factions, who afterward formed different nations– the Pye, the Kanran, and Marmma. The Marmma were the Burmese, and the one interesting point is the tale is that this is the first mention of them. To the above are usually added the Sak or Thet, who were a Chin Tribe, and quite recent census returns still record a handful people who speak Thet.

There was in the time of the Buddha Gautama, a fresh accession of immigrants from India under Daja Raja, and sixteen kings succeeded him. It seems clear that Tagaung (Sakyan line) was dominated by surrounding Shans, from Möng Maw and later from Möng Kawng (the modern Mogaung), as well as from the east, and perhaps still more by successive waves of Kachins.

The last king (Sakyan line) Bheinaka, was overthrown and expelled by the invasion of tribes called Tarök and Taret, from Gandalarit, which, no doubt, is the modern Chinese province of Yün-nan and the invadors were Tai or Shans.

3. (a) What is Buddhism?

by Dr. Nabuo Haneda

Ever since I came to this country from Japan, I have noticed one major difference between American Buddhists and Japanese Buddhists. The difference is that American Buddhists like to identify themselves as Buddhists, saying, "I'm a Buddhist," whereas, in Japan people seldom identify themselves as Buddhists. As a matter of fact, when I lived in Japan, I never said to my friends, "I am a Buddhist."

Every time I hear Americans identify themselves as Buddhists, I have a mixed—comfortable and uncomfortable—feeling about it. I have this mixed feeling because I sense in their words both admirable and erroneous elements. Let me discuss these two elements. First, the admirable element is this: American identify themselves as Buddhists because they take Buddhism seriously, whereas, Japanese do not do so because they do not take Buddhism seriously. They regard Buddhism only as part of their traditional culture; they do not regard it as a personal religion. But, for some Americans, Buddhism is a personal religion, an exciting new religion in which they should be personally involved. This is an admirable element I see in American Buddhists.

Now, let me discuss. What I consider an erroneous element? I feel uncomfortable, when I hear people identify themselves as Buddhists because I sense some kind of religious pride or arrogance. The majority of people in this country are Christians. Thus, people who take up non-Christian religions have a sense of rivalry with Christianity. Some of them believe that Buddhism is superior to Christianity. In order to assert their superiority they say that they are Buddhists, not Christians. But if people use the word "Buddhist to feel superior to others, they are doing something unjustified in Buddhism—

something totally against Buddhism. Buddhism does not allow us to be attached to any form of label or identity, or to indulge in any form of self-love or self-enhancement.

I am not saying that we should not identify ourselves as "Buddhists." It is all right to do so. But we must have a clear idea as to what we mean by the word. What, then, is "Buddhist?" When we say we are Buddhists, how are we viewing other religions such as Christianity? What is the relationship between Buddhism and other religions? Here, I want to discuss these questions.

Since I cannot adequately discuss these questions without referring to my personal background, let me talk about it. In my life, three individuals have exerted considerable spiritual influence on me. I consider them my teacher. Let me start with the first teacher. When I was a junior high school student, I met a teacher, Mr. Keisuke Itoh. Mr. Itoh had difficult experiences when he was young. During World War II, he was a Japanese soldier and was put into a concentration camp in Siberia. He was forced to engage in hard labour there. I heard that many of his friends starved to death. Because of this difficult experience in Siberia, he became a Christian. After he came back to Japan, he became a school teacher. Mr. Itoh was so different from other teachers. When he taught in the class, I could tell that he was searching for the meaning of his own life. He often challenged us to reflect upon our lives. He usually looked depressed and gloomy. So, many classmates of mine, young teenagers who loved cheerful teachers, did not like him at all. He was too serious for them. But somehow I was attracted to this teacher. Since I was very young at that time, I do not think I fully understood him. But I was deeply impressed by the serious manner in which he was teaching us. Because he was a Christian, I became interested in Christianity.

Now let me talk about my second teacher, whom I met,

when I was a high school student. Since I was impressed by Mr. Iroh, a Christian, I started to attend a Christian church, when I was in high school. One day, I attended a class for young adults in the church. There were several high school boys and girls. Since I was attending a boy's high school, and the boys were quite rough, I needed to see some girls at least once a week; this was absolutely necessary for my mental health.

When I attended the class, one cute girl asked, "Mr. Haneda, what kind of novelist do you like best?" This was a tough question, because in those days I was interested only in baseball and fishing. I was not academically inclined at all; I had not read any significant books. But a really cute girl was asking me the question. I had to impress her. I could not say, "I don't read any books." If I had said so, it would have sounded so dumb. So, I seriously thought "What have I read, what have I read?" Then, I remembered that I had read one short by Leo Tolstoy. So, I told her, "Yeah, I, of course, like Leo Tolstoy. He wrote War and Peace and Anna Karenina." (Although I had never read these novels, I knew he wrote them.) She was very much impressed. So it was okay at that time. But it was not okay after that, because she thought I was a specialist on Tolstoy and started asking me questions about him. So, I had to read Tolstoy. I rushed to a bookstore and bought War and Peace and Anna Karenina, huge books. I really thought that I should have told her that I loved O. Henry or Jack London. They would have been much easier to read. But, I said "Tolstoy," so I had no choice. Initially I forced myself to read Tolstoy. Then, gradually I started to love Tolstoy. So when one year had passed, I was more in love with Tolstoy than with that girl. Although Leo Tolstoy is commonly known as a novelist, he was actually a very religious person. When he was around fifty, after he wrote Anna Karenina, he experienced a so-called religious conversion. Most of his later writings were religious writings. I consider Tolstoy my second teacher. So, when I chose my major in college, I chose Russian. I wanted to be a translator of Tolstoy.

Now let me talk about my third teacher. I was in college in the late sixties. In 1969, I was a senior. One day I went to a bookstore and bought a commentary on Goethe's Faust, a famous German story. The commentator's name was Shuichi Maida. I had never heard of him. When I read the commentary on Faust, I was really impressed, not by the story of Faust but by what the commentator Maida said about Faust. Although I had not known it, the commentator was a Buddhist and was interpreting Faust from a Buddhist standpoint. In the books Maida used many Buddhist terms, such as Amida, Sakyamuni, and Shinran. Up to that time, I had no interest in Buddhism at all. To me Buddhism had been part of our obsolete culture. But the Buddhism that I found in Maida was so fresh, new, and relevant to my life. Then, I went back to the same bookstore and bought other books written by him. I started to study Buddhism at that time. That was the turning point in my life. From that time on, for the last thirty years, I have been studying Buddhism.

Now I have talked about the three teachers, Mr. Itoh, Tolstoy and Maida. If I describe them with traditional labels, they are quite different. Mr. Itoh was a Christian. Tolstoy was a Russian novelist. Maida was a Buddhist. But in my mind, I cannot differentiate these three people. They form what I am today.

A friend of mine once asked me, "Mr. Haneda, how did you make the switch? How did you switch from Christianity to Buddhism and from Russian literature to Buddhism?" When I was asked this question, I did not know-how to answer it because I did not feel that I had ever made a switch from Christianity or Russian literature to Buddhism. By getting to know Buddhism, I came to have a deeper appreciation of Christianity and Russian literature. For me, I do not see any conflict in studying Christianity and Buddhism, or studying Russian literature and Buddhism. Actually, studying Christianity or Russian literature is part of my study of Buddhism. For me, studying Buddhism does not mean reading the so-called "Buddhist writings" per se. It means studying all kinds of things, such as Christianity and Russian literature.

To me, Buddhism means realizing an all-embracing attitude, nothing else. It means realizing a broad and empty mind that can encompass all. It means realizing a position in which I can learn and appreciate all kinds of things—a position in which I do not assume any relative or antagonistic relationship with them.

I can talk about this with a simple illustration. Suppose, there is a basket that contains all kinds of fruits such as an apple, an orange, a peach, a pear, etc. To me, religions that have fixed dogmas or creeds are like fruits in the basket. We can compare these religions just as we can compare the fruits in the basket. But Buddhism is not a fruit in the basket; it is itself the basket that holds all kinds of fruits. Buddhism has no fixed dogma, creed, or doctrine. If Buddhism has it, then it can be compared with another dogma. But Buddhism does not have any dogma or creed that can be compared. We can compare an apple with an orange, or an orange with a peach. But we cannot compare an apple with a basket.

Here, some people may disagree with me and say that there are doctrines, ideas and concepts, in Buddhism. Yes, there are certainly ideas and concepts taught in Buddhism. But they are not "fixed" doctrines to be attached or carried around by us. They are cures for sickness. They are something like "Drano" that is used for eliminating a clog in a pipe. When water regains its smooth and nautral flow, "Drano" is no longer necessary. Buddhist ideas and concepts are antidotes against the poison of human attachment. Since we are attached to various objects, Buddhist teachers challenge us with ideas such as "impermanence" and "emptiness" and destroy our attachment. These ideas are totally different from the dogmas that many other religions have.

Let me discuss the basic meaning of "Buddhism" or "Buddhist" by referring to a famous parable about five blind men who attempt to define an elephant. The first blind man touches the tail of an elephant and says, "Now I know what the elephant is. It is like a rope." The second blind man touches its leg and declares that it is like a tree. The third, fourth, and fifth blind men respectively touch its body, nose, and ear and declares that it is like a wall, a hose, and a fan. These five blind men are firmly convinced that they are absolutely right in their understanding. So, they start to fight among themselves.

Then what does it mean to become a "Buddhist" in this context? Here, we must talk about a another sixth blind men. Then who is the sixth blind men? He is a person who touched all those five parts of the animal. He is well aware that the elephant has all kinds of parts. He knows that all those five blind men are both right and wrong. He knows that all of them are right, partially right, because they are touching a part of an elephant. But at the same time he knows that all of them are wrong in their view that they have an absolutely correct understanding. The "Buddhist," the sixth blind men, can identify with all those five blind men, but at the same time, he cannot agree with them when they say that their own respective views are the only truth. Those five blind men have their fixed positions and they cannot help fighting, whereas the sixth blind men has no position with which he can fight with others. A "Buddhist" is a person who can identify with all human assertions in some way or other, but cannot consider any one assertion the absolute truth. The most important thing in Buddhism is the realization of a humble attitude, a broad and empty mind, or an all-encompassing mind. This all-embracing mind is called "Amida Buddha." In the sutra called the Larger Sukhavativyuha-sutra, we read a story in which Dharmakara becomes a Buddha by the name of Amida Buddha. Dharmakara initially vows that he will become a Buddha and create a land, where he will encompass all beings. Then, he takes up practices to become a Buddha. His main practice is visiting and worshipping many Buddhas in the ten directions and studying under them.

The more Buddhas he visits and worships. The humbler he becomes, the more Buddhas he visits and worships. In this way, the number of Buddhas discovers increases. When he discovers innumerable Buddhas and his whole being becomes worshipping and studying, his Buddhahood is fulfilled. He becomes a Buddha by the name of "Namu Amida Bustu (Bowing Amida Buddha)." Here "Bowing" is part of his name. In this way Amida Buddha symbolize the spirit of a perfect student. He has realized and ocean-like mind that can study and appreciate innumerable Buddhas in the ten directions.

In one verse in his Jodo Wasan, Shinran Shonin says, "Taking refuge in the Pure Land of Amida Buddha means taking refuge in all Buddhas." His words meant the following. Amida Buddha is all-encompassing spirit itself. When we go to see Amida Buddha in the Pure Land, we just meet the spirit of a perfect student. In his mind we find only innumerable Buddhas whom he is studying and worshipping. We do not find in him any attachment to his own ideas or thoughts. The contents of mind are "all Buddhas." Thus, Amida is a container of all Buddhas. He just encourages us, just like Amida himself, to discover innumerable Buddhas, visit them, and study under them.

I met my teacher Maida. This does not mean that I have learned a doctrine called Buddhism from him. I have not received any fixed idea or thought from him. The only thing I learn from Maida is the spirit of a perfect student.

He was nothing but student. His humble spirit of a student has challenged all the ideas, notions, and opinions that I cherish. I have been reduced to an ignorant student. I have gained a position in which I can appreciate all kinds of teachers and teachings. He encourages me to discover "innumerable Buddhas in the ten directions" such as Sakyamuni, Shinran, Shakespeare, Goethe, Tolstoy, Dostoevsky, Gandhi and Schweizer, and study under them.

In summary, there are two ways of defining "Buddhism." One is identifying it with a fruit in the basket. The other is identifying it with the basket itself.

If "Buddhism" in a fruit in the basket—a specific doctrine, such as Buddhism is so narrow and limited; it is not the true Buddhism. If "Buddhism" is a doctrine that can be compared with other doctrines, that is a misunderstanding of what Sakyamuni taught. If "Buddhism" means such a limited thing, I do not want to become a "Buddhist". I do not want to called a "Buddhist." But if "Buddhism" means the basket itself, if it means the realization of a broad and empty mind, an ocean like mind, and all encompassing mind, I want to became a "Buddhist." If "Buddhist" means a person who can worship all kinds of teachers and study under them, I want to be called a "Buddhist."

Don't become a fruit in the basket! Become the basket! Appreciate all kinds of fruits in the basket! Buddhism is appreciating all kinds of teachers and teachings. There are so many wonderful teachers and teachings in the world. Let's forget labels such as Christianity, Islam, etc. Let's forget even the labels such as "Buddhism," "Zen," or "Shin." Let us study from all. We are after all, all human beings. We share the same human sufferings and the same human aspirations. We do not have to be trapped by superficial labels and identities.

Ven. S. Dhammika : Good Question Good Answer

4

What is Buddhism

Question: What is Buddhism?

Answer: *The name Buddhism comes from the word 'budhi' which means 'to wake up' and thus, Buddhism is the philosophy of awakening. This philosophy has its origins in the experience of the man Siddhartha Gautama, known as the Buddha, who was himself awakened at the age of 35. Buddhism is now 2,500 years old and has about 300 million followers worldwide. Until a hundred years ago Buddhism was mainly an Asian philosophy but increasingly it is gaining adherents in Europe, Australia and America.*

Question: So Buddhism is just a philosophy?

Answer: *The word philosophy comes from two words 'philo' which means 'love' and 'sophia' which means 'wisdom'. So, philosophy is the love of wisdom or love and wisdom, both meanings describe Buddhism perfectly. Buddhism teaches that we should try to develop our intellectual capacity to the fullest so that we can understand clearly. It also teaches us to develop love and kindness so that we teaches us to develop love and kindness so that we can be like a friend to all beings. So, Buddhism is a philosophy but not just a philosophy. It is the supreme philosophy.*

Question: Who was the Buddha?

Answer: *In the year 563 B C a baby was born into a royal family in northern India. He grew up in wealth and luxury but eventually found that worldly comforts and security do not guarantee happiness. He was deeply moved by the suffering he saw all around and resolved to find the key to human happiness. When he was 29, he left his life and child and set off to sit at the feet of the great religious teachers of the day to learn from them. They* *taught him much but none really knew the cause of human suffering and how it could be overcome. Eventually, after six years study and meditation he had an experience in which all ignorance fell away and he suddenly understood.*

From that day onwards, he was called the Buddha, the Awakened One. He lived for another 45 years in which time he travelled all over the northern India teaching others what he had discovered. His compassion and patience were legendary and he had thousand of followers. In his eightieth year, old and sick, but still happy and at peace, he finally dies.

Question: Wasn't it irresponsible for the Buddha to walk out on his wife and child?

Answer: *It coudn't have been an easy thing for the Buddha to leave his family. He must have worried and hesitated for a long time before he finally left. But he had a choice, dedicating himself to his family or dedicating himself to the whole world. In the end, his great compassion made him give himself to the whole world. And the whole world still benefits from his sacrifice. This was not irresponsible. It was perhaps the most significant sacrifice ever made.*

Question: The Buddha is dead so how can he help us?

Answer: *Faraday, who discovered electricity, is dead, but what he discovered still helps us. Luis Pasteur who discovered the cures for so many diseases is dead, but his medical discoveries still save lives. Leonardo da Vinci who created masterpieces of art is dead, but what he created can still uplift and give joy. Noble men and her heroes may have been dead for centuries but when we read of their deeds and achievements, we can still be inspired to act as they did. Yes, the Buddha is dead but 2,500 years later, his teachings still help people, his example still inspires people, his words still change lives.*

Only a Buddha could have such power centuries after his death.

Question: Was the Buddha a god?

Answer: *No, he was not. He did not claim that he was a god, the child of a god or even the messenger from a god. He was a man who perfected himself and taught that if we follow his example, we could perfect ourselves also.*

Question: If the Buddha is not a god, then why do people worship him?

Answer: *There are different types of worship. When someone worships a god, they praise him or her, making offerings and ask for favours, believing that the god will hear their praise, receive their offerings and answer their prayers. Buddhists do not indulge in this kind of worship. The other kind of worship is when we show respect to someone or something we admire. When a teacher walks into a room we stand up, when we meet a dignitary we shake hands, when the national anthem is played we salute. These are all gestures of respect and worship and indicate our admiration for persons and things. This is the type of worships Buddhist practise. A statue of the Buddha with its hands rested gently in its lap and its compassionate smile reminds us to strive to develop peace and love within ourselves. The perfume of incense reminds us of the pervading influence of virtue, the lamp reminds us of light of knowledge and the flowers which soon fade and die, reminds us of impermanence. When we bow, we express our gratitude to the Buddha for what his teahings have given us. This is the nature of Buddhist worship.*

Question: But I have heard people say that Buddhists worship idols.

Answer: *Such statements only reflect the misunderstanding of the persons who make them. The* *dictionary defines an idol as "an image or statue worshipped as a god". As we have seen, Buddhist do not believe that the Buddha was a god, so how could they possibly believe that a piece of wood or metal is a god? All religions use symbols to express various concepts. In Taoism, the ying-yang is used to symbolise the harmony between opposites. In Sikhism, the sword is used to symbolise spiritual struggle. In Christianity, the fish is used to symbolise his sacrifice. And in Buddhism, the statue of the Buddha also reminds us of the human dimension in Buddhist teaching, the fact that Buddhism is man-centred, not god-centred, that we must look within not without to find perfection and understanding. So, to say that Buddhist worship idols is not correct.*

Question: Why do people burn paper money and do all kinds of strange things in Buddhist temples?

Answer: *Many things seems strange to us when we don't understand them. Rather than dismiss such things as strange, we should strive to find their meaning. However, it is true that Buddhist practice sometimes has its origin in popular superstition and misunderstanding rather than the teaching of the Buddha. And such misunderstanding are not found in Buddhism alone, but arise in all religions from time to time. The Buddha taught with clarity and in detail and if some fail to understand fully, the Buddha cannot be blamed.*

There is a saying.

If a man suffering from a disease does not seek treatment even when there is a physician at hand, it is not the fault of the physician. In the same way, if a man is oppressed and tormented by the disease of defilements but does not seek the help of the Buddha, that is not the Buddha's fault. –JN28-9.

Nor should Buddhism or any religion be judged by those who don't practise it properly. If you wish to know the true teachings of Buddhism, read the Buddha's words or speak to those who understand them properly.

Question: If Buddhism is so good why are some Buddhist countries poor?

Answer: *If by poor you mean economically poor, then it is true that some Buddhist countries poor. But if by poor by you mean a poor quality of life, then perhaps some Buddhist countries are quite rich. America, for example, is an economically rich and powerful country but the crime rate is one of the highest in the world, millions of old people are neglected by their children and die of loneliness in old people's homes, domestic violence and child abuse are major problems. One in three marriages end in divorce, pornography is easily available. Rich is terms of money but perhaps poor in term of the quality of life. Now, if you look at some traditional Buddhist countries you find a very different situation. Parents are honoured and respected by their children, the crime rates are relatively low, divorce and suicide are rare and traditional values like gentleness, generosity, hospitality to strangers, tolerance and respect for others are still strong. Economically backward, but perhaps a higher quality of life than a country like America. But even if we judge Buddhist countries in terms of economics alone, one of the wealthiest and most economically dynamic countries in the world today is Japan where 93 per cent of the population call themselves Buddhist.*

Question: Why is it that you don't often hear of charitable work being done by Buddhists?

Answer: *Perhaps it is because Buddhists don't feel the need to boast about the good they do. Several years ago the Japanese Buddhist leader Nikkho Nirwano received the Templeton Prize for his work in promoting inter-religious harmony. Likewise a Thai Buddhist monk was recently awarded the prestigious Magsaysay Prize for his excellent work among drug addicts. In 1987,* *another Thai monk, Ven. Kantayapitwa was awarded the Norwegian Children's Peace Prize for his many years work helping homeless children in rural areas. And what about the large scale social work being done among the poor in India by the Western Buddhist Order? They have built schools, child minding-centres, dispensaries and small scale industries for self-sufficiency. Buddhist see help given to others as an expression of their religious practice just as other religions do but they believe that it should be done quietly and without self-promotion. Thus you don't hear so much about their charitable work.*

Question: Why are there so many different types of Buddhism?

***Answer:** There are many different types of sugar: brown sugar, white sugar, rock sugar, syrup and icing sugar but it is all sugar and it all tastes sweet. It is produced in different forms so that it can be used in different ways. Buddhism is the same: there is Theravada Buddhism, Zen Buddhism, Pure Land Buddhism, Yogacara Buddhism and Vajrayana Buddhism but it is all Buddhism, Yogacara Buddhism and Vajrayana Buddhism but it all has the same taste, the taste–of freedom. Buddhism has evolved into different forms so that it can be relevant to the different cultures in which it exists. It has been reinterpreted over the centuries so that it can remain relevant to each new generation. Outwardly, the types of Buddhism may seem very different but at the centre of all of them is the Four Noble Truths and the Eightfold Path. All major religions, Buddhism included, have split into schools and sects. But the different sects of Buddhism have never gone to war with each other and to this day, they go to each other's temples and worship together. Such tolerance and understanding is certainly rare.*

Question: You certainly think highly of Buddhism. I suppose you think your religion is

right and all the others are wrong.

Answer: *No Buddhist who understands the Buddha's teaching thinks that other religions are wrong. No one who, has made a genuine effort to examine other religions with as open mind could think like that either. The first thing you notice when you study the different religions is just how much they have in common. All religions acknowledge that man's present state is unsatisfactory. All believe that a change of attitude and behaviours is needed if man's situation is to improve. All teach an ethics that includes love, kindness, patience, generosity and social responsibility and all accept the existence of some form of absolute.*

They use different languages, different names and different symbols to describe and explain these things; and it is only when they narrowmindedly cling to their one way of seeing things that religious intolerance, pride and self-righteousness arise.

Imagine an Englishman, a Frenchman, a Chinese and an Indonesian all looking at a cup. The Englishman says, "That's a cup". The Frenchman answers, "No it's not. It's a tasse". The Chinese comments, "You're both wrong. It's a pet". And the Indonesian laughs at the others and says "What fools you are. It's a cawan". The Englishman gets a dictionary and shows it to the others saying, "I can prove that it is a cup. My dictionary says so". "Then your dictionary is wrong", says the Frenchman "because my dictionary clearly says it is a tasse". The Chinese scoffs at them. "My dictionary is thousand of years older than yours, so my dictionary must be right. And besides, more people speak Chinese than any other language, so it must be a pet." While they are squabbling and arguing with each other, a Buddhist comes up and drinks from the cup. After he has drunk, he says to the others, "Whether you call it a cup, a tasse, a pet or a cawan, the purpose of the cup is to be used. Stop arguing and drink, stop squabbling and refresh your thirst". This is the Buddhist attitude to other religions.

Question: Is Buddhism Scientific?

Answer: *Before we answer that question it would be best to define the word 'science'. Science, according to the dictionary is: "knowledge which can be mad into a system, which depends upon seeing and testing facts and stating general natural laws, a branch of such knowledge, anything that can be studied exactly". There are aspects of Buddhism that would not fit into this definition but the central teachings of Buddhism, the Four Noble Truths, most certainly would. Suffering, the First Noble Truth, is an experience that can be defined, experienced and measured. The second Noble Truth states that suffering has a natural cause, craving, which likewise can be defined, experienced and measured. No attempted is made to explain suffering in terms of a metaphysical concept or myths. Suffering is ended, according to the Third Noble Truth, not by relying on upon a supreme being, by faith or by prayers but simply by removing its cause. This is axiomatic. The Fourth Noble Truth, the way to end suffering, once again, has nothing to do with metaphysics but depends on behaving in specific ways. And once again behaviour is open to testing. Buddhism dispenses with the concept of a supreme being, as does science, and explains the origins and workings of the universe in terms of natural law. All of this certainly exhibits a scientific spirit. Once again, the Buddha's constant advice that we should not blindly believe but rather question, examine, inquire and rely on our own experience, has a definite scientific ring to it. He says:*

"Do not go by revelation or tradition, do not go by rumour, or the sacred scriptures, do not go by hearsay or mere logic, do not go by bias towards a notion or by another person's seeming ability and do not go by the idea 'He is our teacher'. But when you yourself know

that a thing is good, that it is not blameable, that it is praised by the wise and when practised and observed that it leads to happiness, then follow that thing."

So, we could say that although Buddhism is not entirely scientific, it certainly has a strong overtone and is certainly more scientific than any other religion. It is significant that Albert Einstein, the greatest scientist of the twentieth century said of Buddhism.

"The religion of the future will be a cosmic religion. It should transcent a personal God and avoid dogmas and theology. Covering both natural and spiritual, it should be based on a religious sense arising from the experience of all things, natural and spiritual and a meaningful unity. Buddhism answers this description. If there is any religion that would cope with modern scientific needs, it would be Buddhism."

4. The Smaller Sukhavati Vyuha Sutra translated from Chinese by Hisao Inagaki

(1) Thus, I have heard, at one time the Bhagavat was staying in Jeta Grove monastery in Anathapindada's Garden at Shravasti, together with a large company of twelve hundred and fifty monks, who were all Venerable Shravakas and well-known great arhats. They were headed by eminent shravakas, such as the Venerable Shariputra, Mahamaudgalyayana, Mahakashyapa and Aniruddha. He was also accompanied by innumerable Bodhisattvas, Mahasattvas, who were all dwelling in the Stage of Non-retrogression and were adorned with immeasurable merits and virtues, headed by great Bodhisattvas, such as Bodhisattva Manjushri, Bodhisattva Ajita, Bodhisattva Nityodykta and Bodhisattva Anikshipta-dhura. Also in the assembly were a hundred thousands kotis of nayutas (of devas) headed by Shakra along with the King of Mahabrahma Heaven, the Lord of Saha world, as well as the Four Guardian Kings and others. Many demi-gods, innumerable heavenly and human beings,

asuras and others assembled and took their seats to.

(2) The Bhagavat said to Shariputra: "Do you know that if you travel westwards from here, passing a hundred thousand kotis of nayutas of Buddhalands, you come to the land called 'Utmost Bliss,' where there is a Bhagavat named 'Amitayus' or 'Amitabha' with ten titles, including Tathagata, Arhat and Samyaksambuddha. He is living there at this very moment, teaching the profound and wonderful Dharma to sentient beings to give them supreme benefit and bliss.

(3) Why, Shariputra, is that land called 'Utmost Bliss'? Shariputra, beings in that land suffer no afflictions and pain but experience only pure immeasurable joy and happiness. For this reason, that land is called 'Utmost Bliss'.

"Again, Shariputra, in the pure Buddhaland of Utmost Bliss there are seven rows of jewelled balustrades, seven rows of jewelled tala-trees, and sevenfold jewelled nets, which surround everywhere and are completely decorated with four jewels, namely, gold, silver, beryl and crystal. Shariputra, that Buddhaland is full of such glorious adornments of supreme qualities, which are most pleasing to the mind. For this reason that land is called 'Utmost Bliss'."

"Again, Shariputra, in the pure Buddhaland of Utmost Bliss here and there are many seven-jewelled ponds filled with water of eight excellent qualities, namely, (1) pure, (2) cool, (3) sweet-tasting, (4) soft, (5) moistening, (6) comforting, (7) quenching thirst, hunger and many other needs, and (8) nourishing the senses, increasing the activities of the four elements and producing superior goodness. Sentient beings with a large stock of merits always enjoy using such water. The bottom of these ponds is lined with gold sand.

"In the ponds, at all times, lotuses of various colours as large as chariot-wheels are in bloom. Blue flowers

radiate blue light, brilliance and splendour; yellow ones radiate yellow light, brilliance and splendour; red ones radiate red light, brilliance and splendour; white ones radiate white light, brilliance and splendour; four-coloured ones radiate four-coloured light, brilliance and splendour; Shariputra, that Buddhaland is full of such glorious adornments of supreme qualities, which are most pleasing to the mind. For this reason, that land is called Utmost Bliss."

"Again, Shariputra, in that pure Buddhaland of Utmost Bliss limitless exquisite music is spontaneously played at all times. The sound is harmonious and most pleasant to hear. When sentient beings hear its excellent sound, their evil passions are completely removed, numerous good acts multiply and they soon attain the highest perfect Enlightenment. Shariputra, that Buddhaland is full of such glorious adornments of supreme qualities, which are most pleasing to the mind. For this reason, that land is called Utmost Bliss."

"Again, Shariputra, the ground throughout that pure Buddhaland of Utmost Bliss is of true gold. It is soft to the touch and refreshing, shining boundlessly and adorned with rare jewels. Shariputra, that Buddhaland is full of such glorious adornments of supreme qualities, which are most pleasing to the mind. For this reason, that land is called Utmost Bliss."

"Again, Shariputra, in that pure Buddhaland of "Utmost Bliss", six times during the day and night, various heavenly blossoms of rare beauty continuously rain down from the sky. They are brilliant and refreshing, soft and variegated, pleasing to the mind and the senses. They do not rouse greedy attachment, but increase countless inconceivable merits in sentient beings. Six times during the day and night, the being in that land offer those blossoms to Amitayus in homage. Every morning they take those heavenly blossoms and, in such a short time,

it takes for a meal, fly to innumerable other lands to pay homage hundred, to a thousand kotis of Buddhas. They offer to each Buddha a hundred thousand kotis of such blossoms and return home to the pure land, as if to enjoy leisure in a heavenly abode. Shariputra, that Buddha-land is full of such glorious adornments of supreme qualities, which are most pleasing to the mind. For this reason, that land is called Utmost Bliss."

"Again, Shariputra, in that pure Buddhaland of Utmost Bliss there are always many rare species of beautiful birds of various colours, such as swams, geese, herons, storks, cranes, peacocks, parrots, kalavinkas and jivamjivakas. Six timed during the day and night, those birds form a flock and sing with melodious and delicate tones, producing diverse sounds to proclaim numerous wonderful teachings, such as the [four] mindful acts, the [four] ways of stopping evils, the [four] miraculous powers the [five] roots of goodness, the [five] powers, the [seven] factors of wisdom, and the [Eightfold] Noble Path. Having heard their singing, the sentient beings in that land gain innumerable merits through mindfulness of the Buddha, Dharma and Sangha, and their bodies long retain the perfume of virtue. Shariputra, do you think that the birds in that land belong to the evil realm of animals? Do not hold such a view! The reason is that none of the three evils realms, not even their names, exist.

"Again, Shariputra, in that pure Buddhaland of Utmost Bliss soft breezes always blow. When they waft through the jewelled trees and jewelled nets, wonderful sound are produced. As if a hundred thousand kotis of celestial musical instruments were playing together to produce exquisite sounds, when soft breezes which constantly arise in that land waft through the jewelled trees and jewelled nets, they produced various excellent sounds, which proclaim many teachings of the Dharma. Having hard those sounds, sentient beings in that land give rise

to numerous meritorious acts, such as mindfulness of the Buddha, Dharma and Sangha. Shariputra, that Buddhaland is full of such glorious adornments of supreme qualities, which are most pleasing to the mind. For this reason, that land is called Utmost Bliss."

"Shariputra, in that pure Buddhaland of Utmost Bliss there are wonderful manifestations such as those, which are innumerable and inconceivable. Even if a hundred thousand kotis of nayutas of innumerable tongues should praise their excellent qualities for a hundred thousand kotis of nayutas of kalpas, each tongue producing immeasurable voices they would not be able to praise them to the full. For this reason, [that land] is called the Land of Utmost Bliss."

(4) "Again, Shariputra, why is the Buddha of the pure Buddhaland of Utmost Bliss called 'Amitayus'? Because, Shariputra, the life-span of that Tathagata and all beings living there last for immeasurable and innumerable great Kalpas, the Tathagata of that land is called 'Amitayus.' Shariputra, why is the Buddha also called 'Amitabha' ? Shariputra, the Tathagata always emits boundless and innumerable rays of glorious light, illuminating all the Buddhalands of the ten directions without hindrance, so as to display Buddhist ac..."

"Again, Shariputra, the Buddha Amitayus of that pure Buddhaland of Utmost Bliss always has Shravaka disciples, all of them arhats, who are possessed of various excellent merits and whose number is unlimited and incalculable. Shariputra the Pure land of that Buddha is full of such glorious adornments, which are most pleasing to the mind. For this reasons, that land is called 'Utmost Bliss'."

"Again, Shariputra, the Buddha Amitayus of that pure Buddhaland of Utmost Bliss always has innumerable Bodhisattva disciples, all of them in the Stage of Becoming a Buddha after One More Life. They are possessed of

various excellent merits, and their number is unlimited and incalculable. Even if one praised their merits for innumerable Kalpas, one would not be able to praise them fully. Shariputra, that Buddhaland is filled with such glorious adornments which are most pleasing to the mind. For this reason, that land is called Utmost Bliss."

(5) "Again, Shariputra, sentient beings born in that land all dwell in the Stage of Non-retrogression, and will not fall again into an evil realm, be born in a borderland or in the state of debased people or mlecchas. They always enjoy visiting pure lands of other Buddhas. With their excellent vows and practice advancing and developing every moment, they will unfailingly realize the highest, perfect Enlightenment. Shariputra that Buddha-land is full of such glorious merits, which are most pleasing to the mind. For this reason, that land is called Utmost Bliss."

"Again, Shariputra, if sentient beings hear of the glorious manifestations of countless merits in that Buddha-land of Amitayus, they should all awaken aspiration to be born there. The reasons are: first, those born there will meet those Great Beings adorned with such countless merits as mentioned above; second, they will enjoy the pleasure of the Mahayana Dharma intrinsic to this pure Buddhaland adorned with such innumerable merits; and third, with their own immeasurable vows and practice advancing and developing every moment, they will quickly realize the highest perfect Enlightenment. Shariputra, those who are to be born in that Buddhaland do not have few but already countless and unlimited merits, so such sentient beings can attain birth in the pure Buddhaland of Utmost Bliss of the Buddha Amitayus."

"Again, Shariputra, if good men or women of pure faith, having heard Amitayus Buddha's name of innumerable, boundless and inconceivable merits and also heard of the glor..."

"Shariputra, as I perceive that such blissful benefits

are matters of great importance, I pronounce these words of truth: Good men and good women of pure faith who hear Amitayus Buddha's name of inconceivable merits and also learn of the pure Buddhaland of Utmost Bliss should all receive [the teaching] in fait, arouse aspiration, practise the method as prescribed, and attain birth in that Buddhaland."

(6) "Shariputra, just as I praise the innumerable, unlimited and inconceivable merits of the Buddhaland of Amitayus, so do the Buddhas of the eastern direction as numerous as the sands of the Ganges, such as Aksobhya Tathagata, Meru-dhvaja Tathagata, Mahameru Tathagata, Meru-prabhasa Tathagata, and Manju-dhvaja Tathagata. While dwelling in their pure lands of the east, they extend their long, broad tongues and, encompassing with them tthe universe of a thousand million words, pronounce these words of truth: Sentient beings should all received in faith this gate of the Dharma concerning praise of the inconceivable merits of the Buddhaland and protection by all Buddhas."

(7) "Again, Shariputra, there are in the southern direction Buddhas as numerous as the sand of the Ganges, such as Candra-surya-pradipa Tathagata, Yashah-prabha Tathagata, Maharci-Skandha Tathagata, Meru pradipa Tathagata and Ananta-virya Tathagata. While dwelling in their own pure lands of the south, they extend their long, broad tongues and, encompassing with them the universe of a thousand million words, pronounce these words of truth: Sentient beings should all receive in faith this gate of the Dharma concerning praise of the inconceivable merits of the Buddhaland and protection by all Buddhas."

(8) "Again, Shariputra there are in the western direction Buddhas as numerous as the sand of the Ganges, such as Amitayus Tathagata, Amita-Skandha Tathagata, Amita-Prabha Tathagata, Amita-Dhvaja

Tathagata, Maheshvara Tathagata, Mahaprabha Tathagata, Jvalana Tathagata, Maharatna-ketu Tathagata and Sphuta-Rashmi Tathagata. While dwelling in their own pure lands of the west, they extend their long, broad tongues and, encompassing with them the universe of a thousand million words, pronounce these words of truth: Sentient beings should all receive in faith this gate of the Dharma concerning praise of the inconceivable merits of the Buddhaland and protection by all Buddhas."

(9) "Again, Shariputra, there are in the northern direction Buddhas as numerous as the sands of the Ganges, such as Amita-Prabha-Vyuha-Abhijna-Buddhi Tathagata, Mahaskandha Tathagata, Amita-Divya-Dundubhi-Vaishvanara-Virghosa Tathagata, Jaleni-prabha Tathagata and Salendra-raja Tathagata. While dwelling in their own pure lands of the north, they extend their long, broad tongues and, encompassing with them the universe of a thousand million words, pronounce these words of truth: Sentient beings should all receive in faith this gate of the Dharma concerning praise of the inconceivable merits of the Buddhaland and protection by all Buddhas."

(10) "Again, Shariputra, there are in the nadir Buddhas as numerous as the sands of the Ganges, such as Sarva-saddharma-darshana-yukti-sada-jvalana- rajottama-shriprabha Tathagata, Simha Tathagata, Yashas Tathagata, Yashah-prabhasa Tathagata, Dharma Tathagata, Saddharma Tathagata, Dharma-dhvaja Tathagata, Gunamitra Tathagata and Guna-nama Tathagata. While dwelling in their own pure lands of the nadir, they extend their long, broad tongues and, encompassing with them the universe of a thousand million words, pronounce these words of truth: Sentient beings should all receive in faith this Dharma-gate expounding praise of the inconceivable merits of the Buddhaland and protection by all Buddhas."

(11) "Again, Shariputra, there are in the zenith Buddhas as numerous as the sands of the Ganges, such as Brahma-ghosa Tathagata, Naksatra-raja Tathagata, Gandha-prabhasa Tathagata, Utpala-shri-kalpa Tathagata and Sarvartha-darsha Tathagata. While dwelling in their own pure lands of the zenith, they extend their long, broad tongues and, encompassing with them the universe of a thousand million words, pronounce these words of truth: Sentient beings should all receive in faith this gate of the Dharma concerning praise of the inconceivable merits of the Buddhaland and protection by all Buddhas."

(12) "Again, Shariputra, there are in the south-eastern direction Buddhas as numerous as the sands of the Ganges, such as Uttamavipula-megha-ghosa-raja Tathagata. While dwelling in their own pure lands of the south-east, they extend their long, broad tongues and, encompassing with them the universe of a thousand million words, pronounce these words of truth: Sentient beings should all receive in faith this gate of the Dharma concerning praise of the inconceivable merits of the Buddhaland and protection by all Buddhas."

(13) "Again, Shariputra, there are in the south-western direction Buddhas as numerous as the sands of the Ganges, such as Uttama-surya-prabha-yasho-guna Tathagata. While dwelling in their own pure lands of the south-west, they extend their long, broad tongues and, encompassing with them the universe of a thousand million words, pronounce these words of truth: Sentient beings should all receive in faith this gate of the Dharma concerning praise of the inconceivable merits of the Buddhaland and protection by all Buddhas."

(14) "Again, Shariputra, there are in the north-western direction Buddhas as numerous as the sand of the Ganges, such as Amita-guna-jvalanadhpati-prabhasa Tathagata. While dwelling in their own pure lands of the north-west, they extend their long, broad tongues and,

encompassing with them the universe of a thousand million words, pronounce these words of truth: Sentient beings should all receive in gaith this gate of the Dharma concerning praise of the inconceivable merits of the Buddhaland and protection by all Buddhas."

(15) "Again, Shariputra, there are in the north-eastern direction Buddhas as numerous as the sands of the Ganges, such as Asamkhyashata-sahasra-koti-nayuta-vipula-buddhi Tathagata. While dwelling in their own pure lands of the north-east, they extend their long, broad tongues and, encompassing with them the universe of a thousand million words, pronounce these words of truth: Sentient beings should all received in faith this gate of the Dharma concerning praise of the inconceivable merits of the Buddhaland and protection by all Buddhas."

(16) "Shariputra, why is this sutra named 'the Dharmagate expounding praise of the inconveivable merits of the Buddhaland and protection by all Buddhas? Shariputra, it is revealed in this sutra that the inconceivable merits of Amitays Buddha's Land of Utmost Bliss are praised and glorified and that all Buddhas, Bhagavats, of the ten directions, while dwelling in their own lands, display glorious and wonderful manifestations and pronounce."

"Shariputra, if good men or women, who have heard this sutra, now hear or will hear it, have already awakened or will awaken deep faith, they are embraced by those Buddhas, Bhagavats, dwelling in the ten directions, as numerous as ten times the number of the sands of the Ganges. All who practise as prescribed will not regress but will definitely attain the highest perfect Enlightenment and be born in the Pure Land of Utmost Bliss of Amitayus. For this reason, Shariputra, all sentient beings should receive in faith and understand well my words and the words of the Buddhas, Bhagavats, of the ten directions, and should make great efforts and diligently practise as

prescribed. Do not allow any doubt to arise."

"Again, Shariputra, if good men or women have already aspired or will aspire or now aspire to the glorious adornments in the pure land of Utmost Bliss of Amitayus, they will be definitely embraced by those Buddhas, Bhagavats, dwelling in the ten directions, as numerous as the sands of the Ganges, even ten times that number. All who practise as prescibed will not regress but will definitely attain the highest perfect Enlightenment and be born in the pure land of Utmost Bliss of Amitayus. For this reason, Shariputra, good men and women of pure faith should all believe deeply in Amitayus Buddha's pure land of Utmost Bliss and spire to be born there. Do not be indolent."

(17) "Shariputra, just as I now praise and glorify the inconceivable merits of Amitayus Buddha's Land of Utmost Bliss, all other Buddhas, Bhagavats, of the ten directions likewise praise my boundless inconceivable merits, saying: 'How marvellous it is that Sakyamuni, Sakya, Dharma-King, Tathagata, Arthat, Samyaksambuddha, Possessed of Wisdom and Practice, Sugata, Knower of the world, the Unsurpassed, Tamer of Men, Teacher of Gods and Humans, Buddha and Bhagavat, has appeared in this Saha world during the period of the five corruptions: namely, those of time, sentient beings, passions, views and life-span, and that, having attained the highest perfect enlightenment, delivered this teaching, most difficult for the world to accept, in order to guide and benefit sentient beings and give them peace and bliss."

"Thus, Shariputra, you should know that I have appeared in this Saha world of various defilements during the period of the five corruptions and, having attained the highest."

(18) When the Bhagavat had delivered this sutra, all the great Shravakas, such as the Venerable Shariputra,

and Bodhisattvas, Mahasattvas, together with all beings, including innumerable devas, humans and asuras, greatly rejoiced at the Buddha's exposition and received it in faith.

5

A Comparison of Scripts and Languages

Our oldest written record dating from the third century B.C. Asokan inscription which is called Prakrit, stages and its later inscriptions and manuscripts text, we have the Pali (Maghadhese) language of the Buddhist scriptures. The oldest text (not written record) were the collection of the Vedic hymns, the Rig Veda of Aryan-Hindu, who entered north-western India from Persia-Iran about 1400 B.C. (the geographical boundary of India at that time was different). The Sanskrit language, is one of the language used by Brahmins (upper class Hindus). It is called Brahmi letters.

All writing, in fact, is a relatively recent invention. In someway, from the languages, dialect spoken by the people we can trace their migration history and their separation from their root. There language plays a great part in our life and it reveals many things. We have seen the wave of expansion of population from central Asia in ages, inhabiting in inaccessible, remote areas since long. They have spreaded in the north-east region of India and such diverse numbers are not found in any specific area in the world. It will be interesting to note here the modern Assamese language has originated from Indo-Aryan (Prakrit) language, while the independent Assam was ruled by Ahoms who belonged to Tai-Shan race whose language has no relevancy with Indo-Aryan languages. They have been separated from their main stream. The same is the case with the tribes in the north-east region in India.

There are numerous language spoken by various people in this part of the region. The curvic structure of their scripts and the intonations of their languages appear to be very similar. A list of the scripts and languages is given below:

The alphabets of the languages:

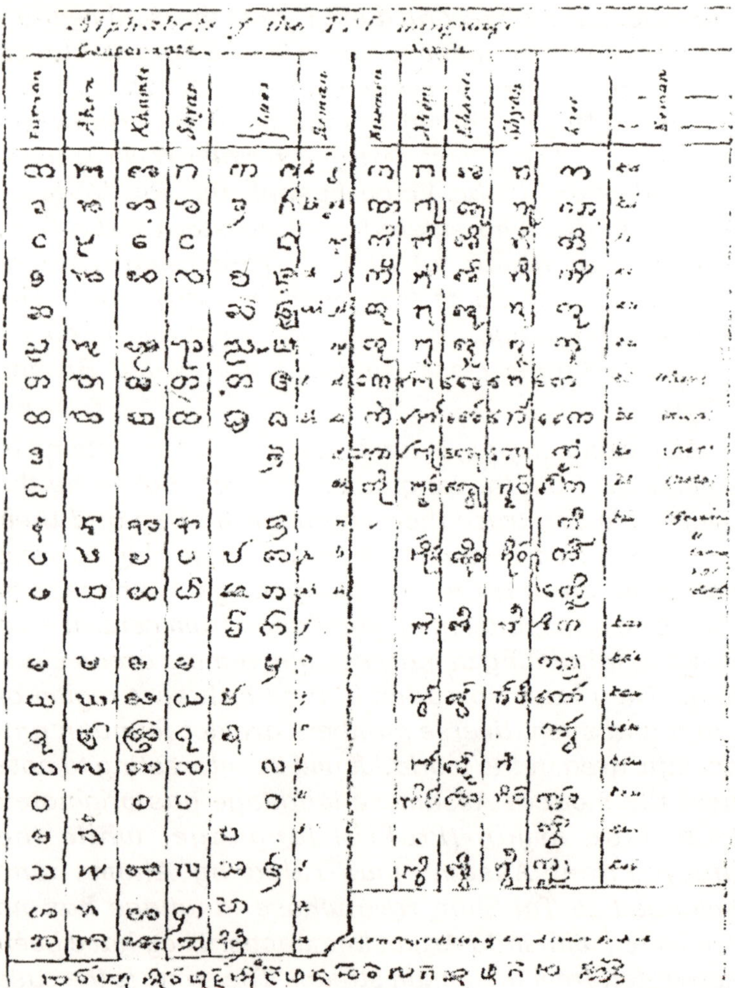

Alphabets of the Chakma Languages

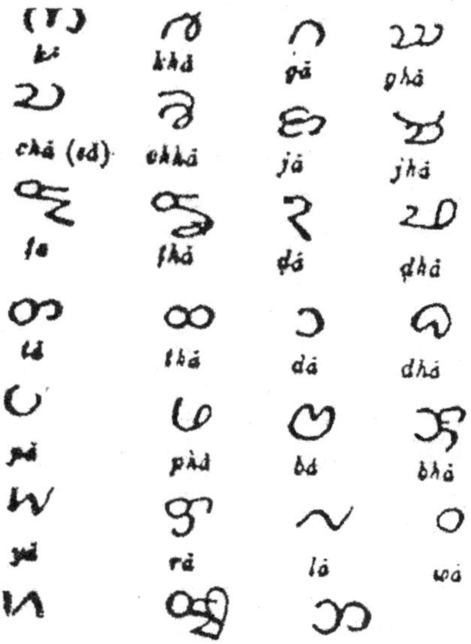

From the look of script developed put of the characters (curvic style) clearly give the impression that they originated from one inscription, which is know Brahmi or Devanagari. The histories of the script of languages are not dealt with appropriately here, as the main idea is to show their common origin. The languages may be more plausible to Pali (Prakrit or Maghadhi) language, which was spoken during Sakyamuni's time. It will be interesting indeed to review how various groups of people interacted each other with associate languages for ages together claiming to be Sakyan.

There might be certain intrinsic and unexplained words whose origin is neither in Sanskrit nor in Pali. The origin of some of the words remained unknown and while considering the meaning of it sematic and syntactic information should be taken into account. A few of them listed below:

* *Yumm (Choom = Jhumm)*: A genetic term of hill where the main stay by slash burning.
* *Toung*: Raised Platform.
* *Toung-thoo*: Hill folks.
* *Phi (Fi):* Spirit resulting unhappiness. The spirit of forests, mountains water etc. it is worshipped in Laos, Vietnam, Myanmar and some other countries. It is also prevalent among the tribal people in Northeast India. The word phi also means the ancestors.
* *Burpara*: Cleanse and make purifying from all evils, spirits, curse, illness, misfortune etc. it is performed by village clergy, usually near the stream of river.
* *Chumulong*: Chaklong traditional marriages with sacrifices of fowls and pigs.
* *Bharbo*: Causing obstruction by spirits.
* *Torbo*: Walking on side steps instead making journey by longer route by boat.
* *Garba*: Household guests.
* *Sageret*: Companion.
* *Pa-thru-thru*: Excellence.
* *Mejang*: Raised stand.
* *Tara*: Devine (Compassion, succor). Helping human being is more in keeping with femininity (motherly). It is not in the goal Therovada branch of Buddhism, instead in Mahayana.
* *U-ba geet*: Love songs.
* *Alam* : Design.
* *Jidu*: Old persons.

The above words might be studied to know the migration history of the group of Sakyans from central Asia to the Himalayan ranges, Hindukush mountain ranges in the last 40,000 years. During the long ages there has been great changes corresponding to languages.

Footnote on development of scripts

It is important to bear in mind that the vast majority across South-East Asia have been poor illiterate and nomadic in those days. Only a handful among the monks could read and write. So it is something misleading to think of the Buddhist books as something to be read in general. There were many developments of Buddhist history of awakening mind by Buddhist monks at the university of Nalanda which was the seat of learning for scholarly monks like Shilavadra, Hueng Tsang, Shanti Deva, and many others of leading light in Buddhism. The voter is of 18 schools gathered together there. It was the gathering of great scholarly monks of that time. It was destroyed by the Muhammedans invasion. The monasteries were sacked and the monks slain, many of the temples were ruthlessly destroyed or desecrated and countless idols were broken or trodden under foot. Those monks who escaped the sword fled to Tibet, Nepal and southern India; and Buddhism as a popular religion in Bihar, its last abode in North India was finally destroyed.

Brahmi

Brahmi: The Brahmi script, found in Asokan inscriptions, which is complete and perfectly legible alphabet, is one of the oldest alphabets that we can associate with the Aryan language of India. The language used in the Mauryan Brahmi script is mainly from of middle Indo-Aryan or Prakrit, but in a few comparatively late specimens we do find Sanskrit used. In course of time the Brahmi script became almost the national alphabet of India, the unbroken development of which we find from about 300 B C down to our day. Various modern scripts of India including those of a number of lands outside India are derivations of Brahmi. The Devanagari, the Bengali-Assamese-Maithili-Newari-Oriya, the Sarada-Gurumukhi, the Tamil-Malyalam, Non-Burmese, the Combodian-Siamese, the Javanese-Balinese and a number of allied scripts in Indonesia are transformations of Brahmi.

A closer study of the provenance of the Brahmi letters found in the Asokan inscriptions shows that the theory of the regional variations is a myth, because as has been shown in the recent studies of the Brahmi script, all the different forms of the same letters may be found in the records of the same region, sometimes even in the same inscription. Therefore, the differences in the forms of letters which we notice are not indicative of regional peculiarities; they were mainly due to the individual stylistic characteristics either in graving of writing the draft that was supplied to and copies by the engraver. Let us give some examples. Notations for A at the top of the initial letters.

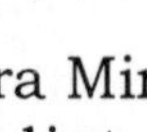

is peculiar to the Gujjara Minor Rock Edict and also to the Major Rock Edict situated about 1600 kilometres from Gujjara, but at Sopara, which is quite close to Girnar, the sign is attached to the middle of the initial letter.

In the Major Rock Edict we notice as many as six forms of Ja

all the prevalent forms of Ra

six shapes of Da

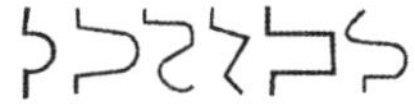

Three each of Ya

and Bha

and both the forms of Ha.

are observed. Almost same is the story of the several letters of the Separate Kalinga Edict found in Orissa, the Bhabru and Bairat Edicts of Rajasthan and the Brahmapuri, Siddhapur, Jatinga-Rameswara and Yerragudi Edicts discovered in Karnataka (Mysore). Therefore, it is now admitted that there are no regional variations in the script of Asoka and that he popularised a standard from of Brahmi, called 'imperial' by A.H. Dani, throughout the country. Form it, it naturally follows that this 'standard' or 'imperial'

Maurya script was confined to only area when Asoka began to make it popular among his people.

The problem may be attacked from another angle, which would also lead to the same conclusion. As is well-known to all students of palaeography and epigraphy, scripts are always in the process of gradual change. In modern times this process has been rather slow because of the bonds imposed upon by the printed forms of letters, but in earlier periods changes in a script were much more swift, so much so that we can determine the age of a document on the basis of its palaeographical peculiarities alone, usually within the limits of few decades. It is, therefore, possible to trace the history of Brahmi from any given point of time onwards or backwards. In the centuries that followed the death of Asoka we find that the engravers of the north began to add little 'ticks' now called serifs to the top of the letters and employ flourishes of various other kinds. The tendency towards ornamentation increased with the passage of time, until the serifs at the top of the letters were joined together in almost a continuous line to form the Nagari script. Other local variations led to the development of other regional scripts in other parts of the country. In Central India in the 5th and 6th centuries a script was evolved which substituted square boxes for serifs of the northern scripts and introduced several others elaborations, while the scripts of the Southern Deccan and Ceylon became more and more circular in form. The Tamils, however, evolved an angular script known as Grantha. Therefore, if one moves up with the line of time, he finds that gradually the regional differences are increasing. And conversely, if he moves backwards in time he finds a gradual decrease in them. But when he moves backwards and reaches the age of Asoka he feels that he cannot go further back, not only because no pre-Asokan documents are available, but also, because he finds that he has reached the point where the script is uniform throughout the country and therefore no more decrease in regional variations is possible. Further the very simplicity and almost primitive angular forms of its letters show a nearness to the time of its invention. Even its orthography as used for Prakrit is not yet complete. Thus, for example, certain consonants are usually not indicated at all (*vassa* being written as *vasa* or *vasa*). Sometimes even reverse forms of letters (reverse *O*

in the Separate Kaling Edict – Dhauli, reverse Dha

in the Separate Kalinga Edict – Dhauli, Separate Kalinga Edict Jaugada, Pillar Edict Delhi- Topara, etc.) are also used. Obviously, its orthography and forms of letters were still somewhat in the experimental stage. Had the history of this script started a millennium or so earlier, we should have found it in a more perfect state and with the some sort of regional variations which we find in it in the age of the Kushanas and the Guptas.

Asokan Brahmi: An Invention of the Grammarians

The fact that Brahmi was invented by somebody and was not the result of gradual evolution is conclusively proved by a study of its relationship is with the Sanskrit grammar. It has been argued with some force that the development of grammar in the pre-Asokan period presupposes the existence of the art of writing. This argument is certainly applicable to those scripts which started as logographic scripts and passed through various other stages. For, it is quite obvious that an ideographic script could have no means of expressing grammatical rules. Therefore, in their case the development of grammar must come later than the development of writing. But in the case of Brahmi it is different. It is now generally admitted that the *varnamala* of this script is a gift of the Sanskrit grammarians. According to Taylor, 'the Brahmi characters represent with absolute precision the graduated niceties of sound which the phonetic analysis of Sanskrit grammarians had discovered................' According to Bühler also the oldest form of Brahmi is, without doubt, a script framed by the learned Brahmis for writing Sanskrit. This assertion is brone out not only by the remnants of the Gaya alphabet of Asoka's stone masons, which is arranged according to phonetic principles, but also by the influence of phonetic and grammatical principles which is clearly discernible in the formation of the derivative signs. According to these scholars and many others, the hand of the Sanskrit phonologist and grammarians is recognisable in the following points:

1. The development of five nasal letters as well as of a complete set of signs for the long vowels. The latter is necessary for phonologists and grammarians but not for men of business, and is, therefore, unknown in other ancient alphabets.

2. The use of separate signs for the phonetically very different but grammatically cognate Sa, Sha and Sa.

3. The notation of U by the half of Va from which the vowel is frequently derived by samprasarana.

4. The non-expression of medial A in accordance with the teaching of the grammarians who consider it to be inherent in every consonant.

5. The derivation of the other vowel signs from the three basic ones, i.e.,

A  I 

and *U*

according to the grammatical rules of guna and vriddhi sandhis. The letter A

is obviously lengthened form of

 , *I* , 

lengthened of *I*

and *U*

is lengthened form of *U*

 and E 

is the result of the *guna sandhi* of *A* and *I*

the strokes of the letter *A* are added to the dots of *I*, *O* is the result of the *guna sandhi* of the medial Ā and *U*

in this case the medial sign of A is placed to the left because we have another letter Ṅa which has the shape of

Ai is formed by adding the medial sign of *A* to *E*

Au is formed by putting a medial sign of A in *O*

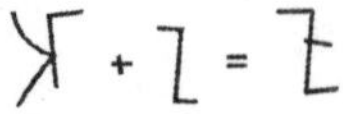

and *Aṁ* is shown by putting a dot to the right of *A*

6. The non-expression of medial A by the difference between Ā and A and of the remaining medial vowels by combinations of the initial ones or the cursive simplifications of the same with the consonants.

7. The use of independent and indubitable signs for all pronounced sounds, identify between pronounced and written letters, separate signs for *anusvāra* and *anunāsika*

 and 

and also for *visarga* and the classification of letters into *vargas* according to the places of their pronunciation.

8. The use of the independent or primary forms for the letters of first and third letters, that is the unaspirated consonants of the each *varga*, other letters of these *vargas*, semi-vowels Ya, Ra and La and Va, sibilants Sa and Sa and the aspirate Ha and the derivation of other letters from them. To some extent this theory appears to be correct. For, the letter *Kha* 

is obviously evolved out of Ga 

Ṅa 

and cerebral Na 

out of dental Na; Chha 

out of Cha 

Ṇ̃a 

out of Jha 

Tha 

and Tha 

out of Ta 

Dha 

out of Da and E 

Ḍha 

out of Ḍa 

or vice versa; pha 

out of Pa 

and Sha 

out of Sa 

Thus, it is obvious that the inventors of Brahmi were very well familiar with the rules of Sanskrit grammar and phonology. In its turn this conclusion proves two points: firstly, as far as Brahmi is concerned, it will not be proper to argue that the development of Sanskrit grammar presupposes the existence of writing. It is the other way round. Secondly, the face that many of the Brāhmi letters are derived from some basic or primary forms means that they were invented at a particular time. They did not evolve from some earlier or more archaic script. Otherwise we would have had different forms for all the letters of Brāhmī. Unfortunately, Bühler, Pandey and Upasak have not given sufficient attention to this aspect of their own researches.

Brāhmi not Derived from the Indus Script

The fact that Brāhmī was invented at a particular time cuts the very root of the theory that it was evolved out of the Indus script. As we mentioned earlier, so far about 2000 Indus seals have come to light. They have yielded some 270 characters (in fact, they must have been far more in number) which were evidently pictographic in origin but probable had an ideographic and syllabic character. But, as pointed out by Diringer, no ideographic-syllabic script became alphabetic without the influence of another alphabetic script. Therefore, Brahmi could have hardly been derived from the Indus script. As regards the vague resemblances between the two, with so many Indus signs to be compared with only about, two dozen primary forms of Brahmi, it is unlikely that there should be no resemblance at all. Further, the existence of such resemblances will not prove anything unless it is shown that it corresponds with not identity of their phonetic values. Moreover, the Asokan Brahmi was read from left to right while the Indus script was read from right to left. The Yerragudi Inscription of Aśokan of which same parts are boustrophedon (reading alternately from right to left and left to right), is certainly a defective document and has no relevance to the question of the origin of Brahmi. Lastly, it should not be forgotten that there is a gap of about 1500 years between the Indus seals and the earliest available Brahmi documents. The existence in the same county of two or more successive scripts does not necessarily prove that one descended from the other. For instance, the early Greek alphabet employed in

Greece and Crete was not derived from the early Cretan or Minoan script of the same area.

Traditional Inventor of Brāhmī

Lastly, there are two more facts which may have some bearing on the problem of the emergence of the art of writing in India. Firstly, the Indian traditions unanimously assert that the Brāhmī was the result of an invention usually ascribed to Brāhmā . It is quite possible that in this story is preserved the echo of a historical fact. On the other hand, it may be nothing more than an attempt to explain the name of the script by concocting a legend which ascribed its creation a Brāhmā.

Need of a Script in the Age of Aśoka

Secondly, it may be noted that the first-half of the third century B.C., when according to our suggestion Brāhmī was invented, was the ripe age for such an achievement on the part of the Indian. Writing is an aspect of culture; therefore, the origin of a script is always connected with a particular cultural context. Now, as is well-known that the cultural life of India was marked by momentous changes during the three centuries immediately preceding the accession of Aśokan. India, in this period, witnessed the progress of the second urban revolution, the rise and expansion of the most extensive empire of ancient history of our country, the advent of money economy, the rise of Vaishnavism and Śaivism, the rise and growth of a number of hetrodox sects and the use of the spoken of Prakr it language as the vehicle of religion. The reign of Aśoka saw the culmination of these tendencies. No wonder, therefore, it also witnessed the greatest invention of the period viz., the invention of writing. After all, the object of Gelb, notwithstanding a script could be created without much difficulty by a culturally advanced people as the Indians of the third century B.C. were. All the necessary conditions for such a big achievement were in existence; they already possessed a highly developed varnamala which was at least as old as the time of Yākṣa (5th century B.C.), the social and political necessities for a script, as we have just seen, were also there the urge for propogating the Dhamma which Aśoka so intensely felt, might have provided the immediate stimulus; and lastly, the familiarity with the idea and use of writing was also present because of India's contacts with literate Greek kingdoms and other North Western regions. In such a situation the learned Pandits of age of Aśoka could easily create a system of writing with help of geometrical forms of pictographs.

Primary Forms are Pictorial Representations of Material Objects

Cunninghan long ago suggested how the forms of Brāhmī letters were created by the Indian scholars. According to him, the Brāhmī letters are the pictorial representations of things and the members of human body which were taken as standing for the first letters of the names of the objects depicted by them. Some examples given by him, specially of the primary letters, are very interesting. Ka, for instance, represents the figure of dagger (Sans. kartari or kṛipā na); Ga of sdy (Sans. gagana); Cha of laddle (Sans. chamas); Ta of three (Sans. tri); Dha of bow (Sans. dhanu); Na of nose (Sans. nasika); Pa of hand (Sans. pāni); Ma of fish (Sans. Matsya); Ra of rope (Sans. rajju); Va of club (Sans. vetra); Sa of snake (Sans. sarpa) and La and Ha of plough (Sans. langala and hala both). If there is some truth in his suggestion it will also go a long way to prove that the forms of

Brāhmī letters were invented at a particular time and, therefore, could not evolve out of any archaic script.

Employment of the Scribes of the North-West

Thus, we conclude that in all probability Brahmi was invented in the age of Asoka and the idea and possibly also the technique of writing came from the West. The advent of a highly developed stone art with strong Iranian affinities but having no antecedents in India proper, offers an exact parallel. There are certain other facts also which indicate Aśoka's indebtedness to the North Western regions in the field of writing. Firstly, the opening formula of the Aśokan Edicts is evidently based on a similar Iranian formula found in the Achaeminic records. Secondly, the very practice of engraving the Royal Proclamations on rocks came from Iran. Thirdly, Aśoka has used the terms lipi (in his Brāhmī inscriptions) or dipi (in his Kharoshṭhī Edicts) which was certainly taken from the Iranian inscriptions. Here it is interesting to note that the terms lipi and lipikara were known to Pāninī who lived in an area which was or had been under Iranian hegemony, but do not occur anywhere in the early Buddhist records. In the Shahabazagarhi Edict, Asoka uses the participles, *likhita, lekhita* and *lekhapit*a which are supposedly derived from the ancient Persian nipish to write. Fifthly, the Kharoshṭhī script, which is generally recognised as derived from the Aramaic script of the Iranian empire, was prevalent in the north-west even in the pre-Aśokan period. And lastly, evidently many of the scribes employed by Aśoka to engrave his Brāhmī records were persons who hailed from the north-west. The scribe named Chapad.a of the Minor Rock Edict found at Brahmagiri, Siddhapura and Jatinga-Rameshvara, who show his proficiency in the Kharoshṭhī script by engraving the word *lipikarena* after *Chapaḍena likhite*, was obviously such a person. The scribe engaged for engraving the Yerragudi Minor Rock Edict must have also belonged to the north west, for he reveals his Kharoshṭhī proclivity by engraving parts of this records in the *boustrophedon* style. And then there are inversions of certain letters noticed in some of the Asokan Edicts which seems due to the old habit of the Kharoshṭhī engravers to write from right to left. All these facts points to the employment of the engravers of the north-west in other provinces including Karnataka (Mysore) in the Far South should not have arisen, but if Brāhmī had been invented in the reign of Aśoka himself, he had no option but to depend mainly upon the artisans from the north-west just as the Gupta emperors had to depend upon the Kushāna mint-masters when they issues gold coins for the first time in the history of indigenous Hindu dynasties.

Analogy of Tibetan Script

In respect of Brāhmī, Aśoka's role reminds us of a similar role which Sron-tsen Gam-po played in the history of Tibet. Srong-tsen Gam-po was a contemporary of Harsha and died in c. 650 after a long reign of about fifty years. He was a conqueror, a law giver and a religious reformer, all rolled into one. He overran western China and Upper Burma and was successful to some extent against Nepal and Assam. He married a daughter of the Chinese emperor as well as a Nepalese princess, the daughter of Aanuvarm. Now until his reign the Tibetan language, though highly developed (it probably had a great epic also), was purely vocal. Srong-tsen Gam-po decided to remove this deficiency in the culture of his country. The following account of his successful attempt in this direction is called from the Tibetan sources:

The king Srong-tsen Gam-po clearly saw that a written language was most essential for the establishment of religion. He therefore sent Thom-mi Saṁbhoṭa with sixteen companions to Kashmir (according to another version to Magadha) and instructed them to devise means for the invention of a written language for Tibetan. He furnished the members of the mission with a large quantity of gold to make presents to the professors. Saṁbhoṭa and his companions reached India and acquired a thorough knowledge of Sanskrit language, Buddhist scriptures and Indian scripts. After returning to Tibet they framed the system of Tibetan writing and composed a grammatical work. The king ordered the intelligent class of people to be taught the art of reading and writing and then required all the subjects by royal edicts to observe ten virtues besides a code of sixteen moral virtues specified by him.

It is needless to observe that the course of events that led to the invention of Brāhmī might have been mutatis mutandis similar in nature. The illustration is too striking too be ignored.

A Possible Objection Answered

Here an objection may be anticipated and answered. It may be justifiably asked if the Indian society was illiterate at the time of the accession of Aśoka, for whom did he get his edicts engraved? Our answer is: partly for the newly educated class and partly for the future generations of his countrymen. In most of his inscriptions he explicitly states that he got them engraved in order to make them long-enduring (chilam thitika cha hotu) so that his progeny shall act accordingly (putra pota cha prapotra cha anuvataram). His emphasis on the use of his inscriptions by his progeny is understandable. So far as he immediate readers of his edicts are concerned, they were probably those who were being instructed in the imperial language through the newly created script. It is not at all necessary to presume that a class of Brāhmī-knowing Indians must have existed long before Aśoka got his inscriptions engraved. After all, apart from a script, he was also using a language which was totally foreign to the common men of a large part of his empire. As is well-known to every student of Indian languages, the linguistic tableau of India had assumed an extremely varied aspect long before the advent of the Mauryas. The Old Indo-Aryan stage of the Aryan speech, as typified by the Vedic or early Sanskrit, gradually transformed into middle Indo-Aryan or Prakṛit. The rate of this change was not the same in every part of the country so that even before the age of the Buddha the existence of three dialectical types in north India are indicated Udichya (North Western), Madhyadesiya (Middly) and Prachya (Eastern). The classical Sanskrit which was later established as a literary language by Panini was based primarily on the Udīchya and Madhyadeśiya dialects. However, in the meanwhile the dialects continued to develop unchecked with the result that the gulf between the two became wider and wider. This was more prominently marked in the East, the land inhabited by the Vratyas (who did not follow the Vedic religion and were adīkshitas or uninitiated people), where Buddha and Mahavīrā used the local dialects to address the masses with the result that they grew as literary languages and became powerful rivals to Sanskrit. Meanwhile in the South, the ancestors of the present Dravidian and also probably Kol (Munḍā) languages were flourishing. The

Dravidian group of languages comprise Tamil, Kannada,Telugu and Malayalam. To this also being dialects like Tulu, Kodagu, Gondi and some others including Brahui of Baluchistan. As E.P. Rice remarks, "nowadays a line drawn from Goa on the West Coast, to Rajmahal, on the Ganges, will approximately divided the Dravidian languages on the South from the languages on the North." In the age of Aśoka the area of Dravidian languages must have been considerably wider.

Against this background the language of the Aśokan Edicts offers an interesting study. It is quite obvious that in his edicts he has used an official languages which must have been the dialect of Magadha. The difference in the inscriptions found in the various parts of his empire are only marginal. The main Magadhan language was used in the Edicts of Rajasthan, UP, Bihar, Orissa, Madhya Pradesh and Karnataka (Mysore). The Rock Edicts of Girnar represent a dialect which has been called western. It is only slightly different from the eastern or Magadhan dialect. For example in the eastern dialect we have l or r (lāja, pulisa)–e instead of final-o (piye, dāne, soche....) and locative singular in-as (is) while the western dialect retains r, ha s and the final o. The locative of nouns is in e and-amhi. The third or the north-western dialect is found in the Edicts of Manshera and Shabhazgarhi. It retains r and has the three sibilants, sh and s also some conjunct consonants. However, there is a marked influence of the eastern dialects both on the western and north-western dialects and, according to S.K. Chatterji and V. Raghvan, the western dialect was derived from the midland speech of the Mathura area.

Thus, the official language of the Aśokan Edicts was eastern or Māgadhi Prakṛit which was only slightly modified for western and north-western edicts. The local variations in the edicts of the various regions are slight that some scholars have divided them into four groups instead of the above-mentioned three, while others divided them into only two groups (eastern and western). But as we have seen the linguistic tableau of India in the age of Aśoka was extremely varied and it is certain that at least in Orissa and southern provinces of the empire the common man did not speak any Aryan tongue. And yet we find that Aśoka has used the eastern official speech in these regions also. Apparently, therefore, the common man of these regions was not expected to read his inscriptions. The same observation may apply to the edicts found in Gujarat and the north-west; for the dialects of these regions also must have differed considerably from the official language used by Aśoka. In other words, speaking from the point of view of language alone, the Aśokan Edicts were not meant for the common man; they were obviously meant for the persons who were being taught the language of the imperial court. In several inscriptions he states it explicitly that these records were meant for the City Magistrates (Separate Rock Edict–Dhauli, Separate Rock Edict–Jaugada-I) Kumāras and Mahāmātras (Separate Rock Edict Dhauli-II) Mahāmātras (Separate Rock Edict Jaugadā -I) and Rājapurushas (Pillar Edict-VII). What is more, everywhere he expects that his officers will explain the messages incorporated in the edicts to the people orally. Obviously, he did not think that the common man will be able to read his instructions himself directly. We, therefore, propose that it was to this educated class of officers and monks, etc., that the newly discovered script was taught and conversely the edicts which were engraved by his imperial command were meant primarily for this class.

References to Writing in the Pāli Canon

Now let us take up the question of the antiquity of the art of writing in India. This question is actually quite distinct and separate from the problem of the origin and antiquity of Brāhmī. For, even if the Indian of the pre-Aśokan period were a literate people, it will remain to be proved that their script was an earlier form of Brāhmī. But did the Indians of pre-Asokan centuries know the art of writing? As we have seen Megasthenes, who visited Pataliputra in 300 B C. categorically states that Indians of his time did not have any written letters. This statement not only agrees admirably with our suggestion that Brāhmī was invented in the reign of Aśoka, but also raises a very strong hypothesis that no script at all was known in the pre-Aśokan India. However, scholars who believe in the hoary antiquity of Brāhmī argue that the Brahmanical, Buddhist and Jain literatures are full of such references which point to the prevalence of writing (which they identify with Brāhmī) in India in the pre-Aśokan period. In this respect the Jain Canon is not of much consequence, because it suffered many violent alterations in the past and the one, claimed by the Svetambaras, was finally settled in its present form a thousand years after the death of Mahāvīra in the Council held at Valabhi in the sixth centruy A.D. As regards the Buddhīst literature, there is no doubt that it contains explicit references to the game of akkharikā (the game of recognising letters written with fingers either on one's own back or in the sky), letters both private and official, written royal proclamations, inapannas or bonds, potthakas or books, pattrakas or manuscripts, lekha or lekhana as a craft and lekhanī or pen, etc. A late Buddhist

Work Lalitavistara preserves the names of as many as 64 scripts (some Jain texts contain the names of 18 scripts only, first of them being Brahmi or Bambhī). According to Bühler, Ojha, Pandey and many others, these references push back the antiquity of writing to the sixth century B C, when Gautama the Buddha flourished. We beg to differ. Firstly, though the history of the Pāli Canon commenced with the First Buddhist Council, which was convened almost immediately after the death of the Buddha in 483 B C, to make a formal collection of his teaching, it was written down for the first time in Ceylon during the reign of Vaṭṭagāmini in 29 B C. Secondly, it is definitely known that many of the Buddhist cononical texts were composed and others probably revised in the reign of Aśoka and this process continued down to the period of Vaṭṭagāmini himself. How, then, can we use the evidence of this literature as an indubitable source for proving the prevalence of writing in the pre-Aś okan period?

Illiterate State of Society in the Pāli Canon

There is also another aspect of the evidence of the early Buddhist literature. It is an indicator of the bias of the supporters of the high antiquity of Brahmī that barrings Rhys Davids, none of them, not even G.S.P. Misra, whose work on the cultural study of the age of the Vinaya has just appeared, has cited those passages and events which positively show that when these books were composed the Indian society was not literate. Firstly, according to the Vinaya texts, the First Buddhist council was convened for the preservation of the scattered sayings of the Master relating to Dhamma and Vinaya by their saṅgāvanā or recitation. Now, the participants of this Council belonged to the highest strata of the contemporary Indian society. They met under the auspices of Ajātaśatru, the king of Magadha. It is also stated quite explicitly that they were very apprephensive of the disappearance of the original teachings of the Buddha.

5. Sankaranayanan : The Origin of Brahmi Script

A Civilization Approach with the Development of Human Progress

Our oldest written record dating from the 3 B C. Asokan inscription what is called Prakrit stages and its later inscription and manuscript text Pali language (Magadhan speech). Assamese is a Magadhan speech. The cultural paradigm of this region. Mongolian background of Tibeto-Burman race. They originated with the union of natives of the land with Scythians from Central Asia. They blended many habits, traits, intrinsic words creeps in their language. In a way, from the languages, dialect spoken by the people, we can trace their migration history and their separation from their root. Therefore, language plays a great part in our life and it reveals many things. We have seen the wave of expansion of population from Central Asia in ages, inhabiting in inaccessable remote backyards since long. The configuration of the mountain ranges has no doubt exercised control over their movements from one region to the another. They have spreaded in this north-east region of India and such diverse numbers are not found in any specific area in the world. There are numerous dialects spoken by various groups of people and a few of them have their written scripts and their into nations of their language appear to be very similar.

David Brandley, La Trobo University: Language Policy and the Typology of Scripts

1. Representations of Tone in Segment-based Scripts

In almost all cases the early versions of a segmental script adapted to another language represent the tones inadequately if at all. For example, the earliest Burmese inscriptions of the twelfth century AD do not use either of the tonal diacritics now used. Indic long and short vowels, where available, were used somewhat inconsistently for one tone distinction; but the other two tones were not distinguished at all. It was only hundred years later that the current system stabilised. For Shan in Burma, it was only in the early 1970s that an orthographic reform introduced the necessary additional tone marks and vowel contrasts missing from the Burmese-derived Lik Tai (Shan orthography).

In many cases the structure of the tones in a language can change radically after the formation of the orthography, as in the case of Tibetan where tonal distinctions have arisen from segmental characteristics such as prefix and initial characteristics, rhyme type and so on. This is also so for languages with tonal systems already indicated in an orthography, as for Thai where various tonal developments related to initial consonant and rhyme types have made the orthographic system with three tonal categories (unmarked, may ek and may tho) quite unlike the various modern systems.

Tonal marking, like other aspects of orthographic reform, can become a matter of controversy. One example is the Protestant Lahu orthography, where the original romanised system of the 1920s used six diacritics and left the low level tone amarked; a revision in the early 1950s which deleted the diacritic for the mid-level tone (thus making it the unmarked tone) and added a postscript lowered hyphen for the low level tone led to considerable unpleasantness between foreign missionaries and among the Lahu Protestants, and has made these Lahu most reluctant to consider further revisions to their script.

A more recent example is among the Ngochang of Burma, where a draft script using postscript consonants to indicate tones and glottal stop (parallel to many 1950s orthographies in China) was prepared in Thailand in the late 1980s. An entire New Testament as well as primers were printed in the early 1990s but then rejected by the community; ongoing discussion and work continues.

In some communities whose scripts were originally developed without marking of tones, speakers have started to feel that some tonal marking ought to be added. For example, the Jinghpaw (Kachin) of Burma are currently discussing whether and how to reform their script to indicate the missing final glottal stop and tones. This may be under the influence of several recently-developed scripts for other languages within the Kachin culture complex, such as Tsaiwa (Atsi), Maru and Ngochang, which use various conventions to indicate these.

For some languages using scripts derived from those which do indicate tones, such as the various Karen and other language of Burma which use extensively modified versions of the Burmese script, the tendency is to use existing tonal indications with similar or different values, and to create further tonal markings as required. The Karen scripts were developed in the mid-nineteenth century by native speakers literate in Burmese working with English-speaking missionaries, and use a range of additional symbols and combinations to represent the different consonants, consonant clusters and vowels as well as the tonal systems. A script derived from the Lao and Northern Thai orthography proposed for Lahu in 1925 also followed this pattern; but it is not now in use. The same procedures have been followed in developing various Thai-based orthographies for minority languages of Thailand; see Smalley (1976) for a number of proposals, most of which have not been put into use. I have also tried developing such Thai-based scripts for two languages in Thailand, Bisu and Gong, but speakers who are already literate in Thai find them different to use unless the orthographic conventions are exactly the same as in Thai.[1]

Tones in Indic scripts

In Bengali and Devanagari scripts adapted to use for Tibeto-Burman languages in South Asia, tones are usually not indicated. In the case of a non-tonal language, as for the traditional Indie script (with an earliest dated inscription in 1113 AD) or more recent Devanagri script used for non-tonal Newari, this of course causes no problems. However for those tonal languages such as Bodo with a Devanagari script or for Manipuri, Dimasha and so on with Bengali scripts, the problem is the same as for various roman orthographies without indication of tones used for tonal languages. Speakers manage to cope, despite the ambiguity; sometimes vowel length or other available or new diacritics are pressed into service. For example, modern Burmese uses *visarga* for one tone and a subscript dot, Burmese *auk myit*, for another.

---

1. This is of course not possible where the phnological systems differ, which is where the problems arise.

In Pyu an extinct Tibeto-Burman language formerly spoken in central Burma, a variety of diacritics and combinations of diacritics is used; the value of these is uncertain but probably relate to tones and if so is the earliest such adaptation, datable to the middle of the first millennium AD and thus considerably preceding the use of tonal diacritics in Thai scripts.[2]

For three varieties of Karen, as noted above, a very extensive modification based on the Burmese system has one unmarked tonal category and a number of mostly innovative postscript diacritics for the other tones. The first scriptures using these orthographies were published for Sgaw Karen in 1839, Pwo Karen in 1845 and Bwe Karen in 1857 (Nida 1972; 220-21). The diacritics used differ: Sgaw uses the Burmese *visarga* and four other symbols, three containing the Burmese version of *viram.* Pwo uses only one of the Sgaw symbols and four others for the tones of oral vowels, using the Burmese *visarga* instead as an indication of one of four tones with nasalised vowels; the other three nasalised vowel tones are indicated by adding the Burmese *auk myit* (subscript dot) tonal indication below the corresponding oral vowel tone symbols.

Tones in Roman Scripts

In the majority of romanisations prepared by missionaries for Tibeto-Burman languages, tones are not represented at all. For example, 40 of 45 such orthographies used for Protestant scripture translationslisted in Nida (1972) do not show any tonal marking.[3] In a few of these language, such as Garo, there are no

2. Pyu has now been replaced by Burmese. Its script is datable to a 2nd century AD variety of Brahmi; the earliest inscriptions, in Sanskrit, date from the late 3rd early 4th century AD (Stargardt 1990: 192, 292) The earliest inscriptions in Pyu are undated; the last is a quadrilingual inscription of 1112 AD with Mon, Pali and Burmese; this is also the earliest dated Burmese inscription.

tones; but most are tonal. In fact, a number of orthographies make use of diacritics above vowels to indicate additional vowels, but only five of those listed use any tonal marking.[3] The first such to be developed was for Lahu, which uses postscript raised and lowered 'v' and inverted 'v' as well as postscript raised and lowered hyphen. This was first formulated in northeastern Burma in the 1920s, and accurately distinguishes all seven tones of Lahu. Participating in this development were some Karen Christians, whose Burmese-derived script indicated the tones with additional postscript symbols, as noted above. The Akha orthography, developed in the late 1930s in the same area, uses exactly the same conventions to represent a parallel five-tone system in a closely related language. Catholic romanisations for Lahu and Akha, developed in Burma after the Protestant scripts, adopt the same solution of postscript diacritics, but use some different diacritics. The Rawang orthography, developed in the early 1950s by a linguistically-sophisticated missionary family, uses superscript diacritics in values more familiar to linguists: acute for high, macron for mid and grave for low tones.

In the Fraser script for Lisu, the six tones are indicated by one of six combinations of punctuation marks (. , ., .. : ;) after each syllable punctuation must thus be indicated otherwise. The unused Fraser script for Naxi uses similar conventions.

Unlike these Christian orthographies, all of the numerous romanisations developed in China after 1950 consistently use postscript consonants to indicate tones. It is sometimes suggested that this convention was first developed in nineteenth century

---

3. Of course a number of romanisations developed since 1972 do indicate tones in various ways.

attempts by missionaries to represent non-Mandarin varieties of Chinese; but it was only systematised and widely applied by linguists with the approval and support of the Chinese government in the 1950s and afterwards. Where necessary, a final glottal stop or creaky voice is indicated by a final consonant; this is followed by the letter representing the tone, with one tone left unmarked. In compounds, where ambiguity would otherwise exist the break between a tone-marking consonant and a following syllable is indicated by an apostrophe. Digraphs are preferred to non-roman symbols for consonants and vowels. While syllables and words may thus look long and phonetically strange, such conventions have the major advantage that speakers with imperfect literacy skills do not tend to omit the tones; conversely, in those Christian scripts which use postscript or superscript diacritics (Lahu, Akha, Rawang and Lisu), I have observed that speakers often do omit them when writing.

Unfortunately, the values of the tones indicated by the same postscript consonant differ from orthography to orthography in China. Another problem is that the syllable-separating apostrophe is often omitted, as speakers can disambiguate from context. In a few cases, not all tones were indicated in the first versions of these orthographies; for example, two distinct tones (low level and low falling) were both indicated by a postscript *-l* in the first version of the Chinese Lahu orthography. This omission was eventually corrected with a script reform in 1989 which added *-f* for the low level tone (as well as distinct digraphs to distinguish high and mid-central unrounded vowels); for full details, see Bradley (1994). Several other romanised scripts have undergone similar minor reform in the 1980s, and additional romanised scripts continue to be introduced in China.

2. The following table Showing some of the local words spoken by the four different tribes of Tibeto-Burman race.

Sl. No. (Karen)	*English*	*Myanmar (Burmese) (Tat-Shan)*	*Mug (Arakanesse)*	*Chakma*	*Chakma (Anakya)*	*Manipuri (Doing-Nak)*	*Manipuri*	*Syam (Matte)*	*Simpho (Bishnupriya)*	*Ahom Tat*
1.	Air	Lee	Leei	Boair	Bo	Nungshit	Bo.	Lum	Umbung	Lum
2.	Ant	Paynetseik	Praw-chee	Pigira	-	Kakching	Pipara	Mut	Gugin	Nyasu
3.	Arrow	Mya	Hleek	Tir	Le	Ten	Tir	Kang	Pla	Klang
4.	Bird	Nget	Hngak	Pek	-	Uchek	Phakiya	Nuk	Who	Nuk
5.	Blood	Thwe	Sweei	Lo	-	E	Rokot	Leut	Sai	Leut
6.	Boat	Hle	Hleei	Na	No	Hi	Now	-	Li	-
7.	Bone	Ayo	Arrow	Ar	Ar	Sharu	ar	Dak	Ngrang	Duk
8.	Buffalo	Kyue	Quei	Mosh	Mo-it	E roi	-	Khai	Nga	Khari
9.	Cat	Kyaung	Kraung	Belei	Bi-lai	Houdong	Mekori	Mew	Ningyow	Meu
10.	Cow	Nwa	Nowa	Goru	Go-ru	Shan	Gai	Who	Gongsu	Hu
11.	Day	Ne	Rauk	Din	Din	Nungdhan	Din	Ban	Chingney	Ban
12.	Dog	Khwe	Khweei	Kugur	Ku-gur	Hui	Kukur	Ma	Gui	Mateng
13.	Ear	Na	Nau	Kan	Kan	Kankong	Kan	Phiu	Nae	Pik
14.	Earth	Mye	Pithming	Pithivi	-	Prithvi	Prithvi	Mung-kang	Ngaga	Langdin
15.	Egg	U	Beo	Booda	-	Yerum	Dim	Kai	Di	Khai
16.	Elephant	Sheu	Chhang	Edh	-	Shamu	Aahti	Chang	Mugui	Chang
17.	Eye	Myetse	Myaukchi	Chook	Sop	Mit	Mikhi	Huita	Mee	Taa
18.	Father	A-phe	Aapha	Bap	Bap	Mapa/Epa	Bapok	Poo	Aowa	Poman
19.	Fire	Mi	Ming	Aagun	A-gu-in	Mei	Cn	Phan	Wan	Phai
20.	Fish	Nga	Ngaa	Mash	Mait	Nga	Mash	Pa	Ngasun	Pla
21.	Flower	Pass-bwen	Peng	Ful	-	Lei	Ful	Bokja	Suban	Blok

22	Foot	Khye	Kophwa	Teng	Teng	Khong	Teng	Tin	Kokong	Khao
23	Goat	Sheik	Chhoi	Chagal	Sa-gol	Hameng	-	Pangya	Ponam	Pengnga
24	Hai	Shaben	Chengbaung	Chul	Sul	Masm/Sam	Chul	Fum	Kra	Phrum
25	Hand	Let	Alau	Haat	Hat	Khut	Aath	Moo	Latah	Muo
26	Head	Khaung	Ageng	Sira	Tsir-ra	Kok	Mur	Hu	Bong	Ru
27	Hog	Wet	Wauk	Sugor	Sagor	Ok	Ho-or	Mao	Wah la	Mu
28	Horn	Khyo	-	Singh	-	Machi	Hing	Khaw	Rung	Khaw
29	Horse	Myen	Mraung	Gora	Gor-ra	Sagol	Gora	Mae	Khumrang	Maa
30	House	Eing	Ing	Ghar	Gur	Yum	Gor	Hum	Untah	Reum
31	Iron	Than	Seng	Loha	Lo-a	Yot	Loha	Lik	Imphri	Lik
32	Leaf	Yuet	Phaurwa	Pada	-	Mana	Pats	Bau	Luo	Bao
33	Light (Dawn)	Len	Alang	Bannei/pattya	-	Ayuk	Bian	Khoi	-	Ngaoi
34	Light	-	Alang	Phor	-	Mangar	-	-	Thai	Deut
35	Man	Lu	Yaukya	Marod	Morot	Me	Manoh	Kun	Lasha	Kun
36	Monkey	Myauk	Myauk	Bandar	-	Yong	Banar	Liling	Woie	Ling
37	Moon	La	Laba	Chan	Then	Tha	Chaad	Dunnow	Sta	Deun
38	Mother	Ame	Aming	Ma	Ma	Ema	Manak	Mea	Anu	Meman
39	Mountain	Taung	Mrauing-hmodaung	Mura	Mu-ra	Ching	-	Doi	Bow	Doy
40	Mouth	Uhok-payat	Khonang	Muh	-	Chin	Oath	Sup	Lungup	Naa
41	Mosquito	Khyeen	Kharang	Moja	-	Kang	Moha	Jung	Zee	Neving
42	Name	Name	Amei	Nang	-	Ming	Nang	Chu	Ming	Chuo
43	Night	Nya	Ngwei	Rait	Rait	Chingdhung	Rati	Kham	Zing nah	Kheun
44	Oil	Tsi	Chheik	Tel	-	Thao	Tel	Naman	Namin	Nam man
45	Plantain	Nghet-pyo	Ngaukpi	Kola	Ko-la	Laphoi	Kola	Kui	Nungo	Kuyn
46	River	Myit	Khyaung	Gang/chora	Gang	Turen	Nodi	Namlung	Kannu	Khe
47	Road	Lan	Leng	Padh	-	Lampi	Path	Kunglang	Lum	Tang

48	Salt	Sha	Chha	Nun	-	Thum	Nun	Ku	Chum	Ku
49	Skin	Tha-ye	Arree	Cham	-	Unsha	Chamra	Nang	Fie	Nang
50	Sky	Mo	Gaung-khawng	Deba	-	Atia	Aakash	Kang hoo	Muh	Phaa
51	Snake	Myue	Mring	Sap	Tsap	Lin	horop	Ngun	Lupon	Ngun
52	Star	Kye	Kri	Tara	Tara	Thawamacha	Tara	Dau	-	Dao
53	Stone	Khayuk	Kyauk	Sil	Sil	Nung	Pathar	Hin	Nglung	Rin
54	Sun	Ne	Ning	Bel	-	Numil	Suja	Wan	Jaan	Baan
55	Tiger	Kya	Kyaa	Bug	-	Kei	Bue	Su	Suorong	Suo
56	Tooth	Thaw	Swa	Daath	-	Ya	Death	Khiu	Wa	Khiu
57	Tree	Thit-pen	Apang	Gaach	Ga-it	Pambi	Sopah	Tunmai	Phunban	Tun
58	Village	Yua	Paucho	Adaam	Para	Khung gang	Gang	Ban	Mereing	Baan
59	Water	Ye	Ri	Pani	Pani	Eshing	Pani	Nam	Kha	Nam
60	Yam (sweet) Potato)	Myak-khaung	Mraw	Suguri alu	A-lu	Mangra	-	Manwan	-	Manbaan

The following table showing some of the local words spoken by different tribes of Tibeto-Burman race

Sl. No.	English	Myanmar (Burmese)	Mug (Arakanesse)	Chakma (Anakya)	Chakma (Boing-Nak)	Manipuri (Maite)	Manipuri (Bishnupriya)	Syam-Tai (Karen)	Simpho (Tai-Shan)	Ahom No.
1.	Air	Lee	Leei	Boair	Bo	Nungshit	Bow	Lum	Umbung	Lum
2.	Ant	Paynetseik	Praw-chee	Pigira	-	Kakching	Pipara	Mut	Gugin	Nyasu
3.	Arrow	Mya	Hleek	Tur	Le	Ten	Tir	Kang	Pla	Klang
4.	Bird	Nget	Hngak	Pek	-	Uchek	Phakiya	Nuk	Who	Nuk
5.	Blood	Thew	Sweei	Lo	-	E	Rokot	Leut	Sai	Leut
6.	Boat	Hle	Hleei	Na	No	Hi	Now	-	Li	-
7.	Bone	Ayo	Arrou	Ar	Ar	Sharu	Aar	Duk	Narang	Duk
8.	Buffalo	Kyue	Quei	Mosh	Mo-it	E roi	-	Khai	Nga	Khrai
9.	Cat	Kyaung	Kraung	Bi-lai		Houdong	Mekori	Mew	Ningyow	Meu
10.	Cow	Nwa	Nowa	Goru	Go-ru	Shan	Gai	Who	Gongsu	Hu
11.	Day	Ne	Rauk	Din	Din	Nungdhan	Din	Ban	Chingney	Ban
12.	Dog	Khwe	Khweei	Kagur	Ku-gur	Hui	Kukur	Ma	Gui	Mateng
13.	Ear	Na	Nau	Kan	Kan	Nakong	Kan	Phiu	Nae	Pik
14.	Earth	Mye	Pithming	Pithivi	-	Prithvi	Prithvi	Mungkang	Ngaga	Langdin
15.	Egg	U	Beo	Booda	-	Yerum	Dim	Kai	Di	Khai
16.	Elephant	Sheu	Chhang	Edh	-	Shamu	Aahti	Chang	Mugui	Chang
17.	Eye	Myetse	Myaukchi	Chook	Sop	Mit	Akhi	Huita	Mee	Taa
18.	Father	A-phe	Aapha	Bap	Bap	Mapa/Epa	Bapok	Poo	Aowa	Poman
19.	Fire	Mi	Ming	Aagun	A-gu-in	Mei	Gi	Phai	Wan	Phai
20.	Fish	Nga	Ngaa	Mash	Mait	Nga	Mash	Pa	Ngasun	Pla
21.	Flower	Pass-bwen	Peng	Ful	-	Lei	Ful	Bokja	Suban	Blok
22.	Foot	Khye	Kophwa	Teng	Teng	Khong	Teng	Tin	Lokong	Khao
23.	Goat	Sheik	Chhoi	Chagal	Sa-gol	Hameng	-	Pangya	Ponam	Pengnga
24.	Hair	Shaben	Chengb-aung	Chul	Sul	Masam/ Sam	Chul	Fum	Kra	Phrum
25.	Hand	Let	Alau	Haat	Hat	Khut	Aath	Moo	Latah	Muo
26.	Head	Khaung	Agong	Sira	Tsir-ra	Kok	Mur	Hu	Bong	Ru
27.	Hog	Wet	Wauk	Sugor	Sugor	Ok	Ho-or	Mao	Wah la	Mu
28.	Horn	Khyo	-	Singh	-	Machi	Hing	Khaw	Rung	Khaw
29.	Horse	Myen	Mraung	Gora	Gor-ra	Sagol	Gora	Mae	Khumrang	Maa

30.	House	Eing	Ing	Ghar	Gur	Yum	Gor	Hun	Untah	Reun	
31.	Iron	Than	Seng	Loha	Lo-a	Yot	Loha	Lik	Imphri	Lik	
32.	Leaf	Yuet	Phaurwa	Pada	-	Mana	Pata	Bau	Lup	Bao	
33.	Light(Dawn)	Len	Alang	Bannei/ pattya	-	Ayuk	Bain	Khoi	Nagaoi	Nagaoi	
34.	Light	-	Alang	Phor	-	Mangan			Thai	Deut	
35.	Man	Lu	Yaukya	Marod	Morot	Me	Manoh	Kun	Lasha	Kun	
36.	Monkey	Myauk	Myauk	Bandar		Yong	Banar		Liling	Woie	Ling
37.	Moon	La	Laba	Chan	Than	Tha	Chaad		Dunnow	Sta	Deun
38.	Mother	Ame	Aming	Ma	Ma	Ema	Manak	Mea	Anu	Moman	
39.	Mountain	Taung	Mraung-hmodaung	Mura	Mu-ra	Ching	-	Doi	Bow	Doy	
40.	Mouth	Uhok-payal	Khonang	Muh	-	Chin	Oath	Sup	Lungup	Naa	
41.	Mosquito	Khyeen	Khrang	Moja	-	Kang	Moha	Jung	Zee	Neying	
42.	Name	Name	Amei	Nang	-	Ming	Nang	Chu	Ming	Chuo	
43.	Night	Nya	Ngwei	Rait	Rait	Nung dhang	Rati	Kham	Zing nah	Kheun	
44.	Oil	Tsi	Chheik	Tel	-	Thao	Tel	Naman	Namin	Nam man	
45.	Plantain	Nghet-pyo	Ngaukpi	Kola	Kola	Laphoi	Kola	Kui	Nungo	Kuyn	
46.	River	Myit	Khyaung	Gang/chora	Gang	Turen	Nodi	Namlung	Kannu	Khe	
47.	Road	Lan	Leng	Padh	-	Lampi	Path	Kungtang	Lum	Tang	
48.	Salt	Sha	Chha	Nun	-	Thum	Nun	Ku	Chum	Ku	
49.	Skin	Tha-ye	Arree	Cham	-	Unsha	Chamra	Nang	Fie	Nang	
50.	Sky	Mo	Gaung-khawng	Deba	-	Atia	Aakash	Kang hoo	Muh	Phaa	
51.	Snake	Myue	Mring	Sap	Tsap	Lin	Horop		Ngun	Lupoh	Ngun
52.	Star	Kye	Kri	Tara	Tara	Thawam-acha	Tara	Dau	-	Dao	
53.	Stone	Khyauk	Kyauk	Sil	Sil	Nung	Pathar	Hin	Nglung	Rin	
54.	Sun	Ne	Ning	Bel	-	Numit	Suja	Wan	Jaan	Baan	
55.	Tiger	Kya	Kyaa	Bug	-	Kei	Bug	Su	Suorong	Suo	
56.	Tooth	Thaw	Swa	Daath	-	Ya	Death	Khiu	Wa	Khiu	
57.	Tree	Thit-pen	Apang	Gaach	Ga-it	Pambi	Sopah		Tummai	Phunban	Tun
58.	Village	Yua	Paucho	Adaam	Para	Khung gang	Gang	Ban	Mereing	Baan	
59.	Water	Ye	Ri	Pani	Pani	Eshing	Pani	Nam	Kha	Nam	
60.	Yam (sweet potato)	Myak-khaung	Mraw	Suguri alu	A-lu	Mangra	-	Manwan	-	Manbaan	

The following table showing some words spoken by the four the different groups of ethnic people.

English Words	*Chakma*	*Ayam/Asom*	*Manipuri (Bishnupriya)*	*Turung (Shyam)*
1. Earth/Universe	Pithimi/Jagat	Mati, Jagat	Jagat	Mung kangga
2. Land	Madi, Bhui,	Mati, Bhumi	Be-bee	Ēnga
3. Air	Baiyar	Bayu, Boota	Bau	Ōmbung
4. Sun	Bel	Beli, Hurzyo	Beli	Zaan
5. Sunrise	Bel-Udhana	Beli Uday	Beli-go-kana	Zaan Pru
6. Sunset	Bel-Dubana	Beli-thera	Beli-go-hamani	Zaan Yuk
7. Sunlight	Bel-O-Sadak	Akash-Biman	Belighar-pahar	Zaan Zaa
8. Solar Eclipse	Bel-Gandha	Harzyo-grahan	Belir-garan	—
9. Sky	Aghaj, Deba	Akax, biman	Hagh	Muh
10. Heat	Dap, ōom, Um	Gorom, Tapot	Tabtāa	Kēthat
11. Moon	Jun, Chan	Jun, Chandra	Innak	Sta
12. Moon light	Jun-Pahar	Junhr-Pahar	Junakar-Pahar	—
13. Star	Tara	Tora, Thoba	Tera	—
14. Cool	Zōoro	Shital Size	ing	Chie
15. Water	Pani, Panee	Panee	Pani, Pañee	Khā
16. Sea	Doorza	Xagar	Samundra	Kham
17. River	Gang	Nei, Nodi	Khong	Kham
18. Thunder	Thadhal	Gajanee	Bajra	—
19. Stream	Chara, Bhap	Strot, Bhap	Nala, Chara	—
20. Flood	Gulopani-ban	Banpani	Gala	Khaktung
21. Snow	Him	Him Shila	Baraph	Baraph
22. Lake	Maini, Dheba	Bit, Hrod	Chera, Bil	—
23. Cloud	Megh	Megh, Daor	Meghale	—
24. Sand	Koroli	Dhuli, Bali	Leng-u-Lenyu	Kum chai
25. Hills	Mura	Maru	Tengara	Bhum
26. Fog	Khu-a	Kuhali	Khu-a/Khuja	—
27. Forest	Tarum	Bon/Habi	Jangle/Bon	Nam
28. Valley	Mon-tuli	Upataka	Thawl	—
29. Night	Redh	Rati, Nekha	Rati	Snah

6
A Vision of Reality

All the creations in this universe are living in harmony (holistism philos). A trivial disharmony in nature would result a vast devastation (unhappiness, miseries). It is, therefore, a very complex system, where science can never provide all complete and definitive understanding. Our modern civilization has distabilised this harmony in the last one century even more, resulting the sea level rise by almost one metre, displacing 7.5 million people and 4200 roads. Recently, there was Tsunami (large wave produced by earthquake. Everything is existing synchronously, ecologically. This consciousness, awareness is passing through the nerve and the energy of natures is known as mind. This works in Yogo (physiotheraphy, Pranic healing, Holistic healer, Naturopathy, Reiyukia (Pali word) (Japan) and in Buddhism (dhyom skt) Vipasana in Therovada and Zen (silence) Chittaviyeka-Scanning mind).

Buddhism deals with developing mind (insight meditation) by individual efforts, through absorbtion of ones mind to reach the highest (supreme). Every human being is born with full potentials for developing towards this goal.

Buddhás Mogharaja Sutta (emptyness) says be mindful, see the world is void–having eradicated the notion of an Atma–so many one overcome death–Atma is ego.

The sharpen mind is known as beautiful mind understanding that the minutest particle is called Atom and when two atoms are existing, these must be an intervening space (a notion of space). In this space, we find the attraction and repulsion at the same time. The intervening space is found to be the most potential state of energy, awareness in mind. Thus, mind is a current of energy passing through the nerves and every nerve is made for one single idea and as they have innumerable ideas of compound and complex form and our nerves are innumerable as to give currency of ideas. The ideas are the manifestation of energy.

In general people prefer developing a faith as a process of inductive reasoning. The other method or way is called deductive reasoning, discursive which is based on systematic analysis. Sakyamuni preached in Kalama Sutta:

"Do not believe anything because it is believed by parents, teachers, learned men, men of high rank or the public or because it is thought to be given divine inspirations, or by and oracle, or because it is handed down by traditions, or because it is found in book, or because someone proclaims it to be true, but believe anything if it agrees with reasons investigation and experienced knowledge."

The human beings like the animals (beast) gratifying one's own desire in similar manner because, they are the product of the same ethical matters (air, fire, water and earth): but human beings have the faculty of vision, consciousness, awareness, perception, action in mind. A precise way of discribing the enticement in nature's way: For Deer by music; For Fish by taste; For Bees by smell; For Moth by light; and For Elephant by Lust.

Human beings are also being enticed by all these elements. The planet (earth) on which we dwell, is the hiding place of fox, badger, etc.

Human beings basically are blessful in ignorance,

obscure mind (avidya). But one can get off from it by mind power like the pearls. It is wisely said there has to be a grit in the oyster, which often produces pearls. The grit symbolizes dukkha and to be wise one has to liberate oneself from the grit through a vision of reality.

To dispel the clouds of ignorance, which, like a thick mist, encompasses all sentient beings, and shed bright rays of pure light, which enlighten the understanding. Below in quoted from His Holiness, The Dalai Lama:

"Whether one believes in a religion or not, and whether one believes in rebirth or not, there is not anyone who does not appreciate kindness and compassion."

Mahayana School (Greater Vehicle) of Buddhism involves in Bhakti (devotion + intelligence). It has three main mantras (swim and stream):

1. NA MU MYO HO RENGE KYO; Lotus flower teaching;
2. NA MU AMIDA BUTU; Amida Buddha, JODO in Japan
3. O MAN PEME PUM; Aolokitesvara, in Japan.

Buddhism is being practised in various forms and the unfamilraity of its teaching can sometimes become confusing to general masses. There can be many interpretations of the Buddha, his breaching, teaching and the Buddhist Community. As a result, Buddhist have a wide range of practices and ideas. Buddhism is, in fact, not a hierarchical organisation. It shows the path of purity–self-enlightenment (wisdom), by getting off from the grip of basic delusion and self passion by prespicacious reasoning (a vision of reality).

In deep sense the term of 'Meditation' in the west

may mean 'Dhyana', but it is not corresponding to Sakyamuni's Jhāna Buddhist Jhāna and Yogo Dhyana may have common root in India's remote past, but the latter one has Vedic doctrine, but Jhana is preparing and not an end in itself in Buddhism concentration, absorbtion)

Human Mind: It is the self-guiding and self regulating machine of the system value in life thinking. It is called cognitive science (mental process). The thinking in mind is in constant flux (pulpitating) like lighting, illusion, foam and abstraction. Mind is an energetic effort obstinacy, equanimity and concentration. It negotiates in active ways. It can also develop serenity in mind, thinking with mind and body; mind and brain. In order to gain higher mental training in a monk's life in Buddhist system, there should be development of serenity in body and brain of the man who devotes on holistic tendency to tread. Mind has also thermochemical devises that generates heats in a part of a body.

1. Ignorance:

Nyanatiloka: Buddhist Dictionary

"Through Ignorance are conditioned the Karma-formations" (*avijjā-paccayā sankhārā*), i.e., all wholesome and unwholesome actions (Karma, q.v.) of body, speech and mind, are conditioned through ignorance. By 'Karma-formations' are meant karmically wholesome and unwholesome volitions (*cetanā*), or volitional activities, in short Karma (q.v., and Fund, II).

In view of the many misconceptions current in the West, it is necessary to repeat here that Karma (q.v.), as a technical term, never signifies anything but moral or immoral action, i.e. the above-mentioned volitional activities, or Karma-formations, as either causing results in the present life or being the causes of future destiny and rebirth. Thus, Karma, as a philosophical term, never means the result of action, as often wrongly conceived by Western authors.

Now, in what way are the Karma-formations conditioned through Ignorance? As concerns the unwholesome Karma-formations associated with greed, hate or delusion (*lobha, dosa, moha*), these are always and in all circumstances, conditioned through the simultaneous ignorance inseparably associated therewith. Thus, ignorance is for the unwholesome Karma-formations a condition by way of Conascence (*sahajāta-paccaya*), Association (*sampayutta-paccaya*), Presence (atthipaccaya) etc.— Ignorance further may be for them a condition by way of Decisive Support or Inducement (*upanissaya-paccaya*), if, for instance, Ignorance coupled with Greed, induces a man to commit evil deeds, as killing, stealing, unlawful sexual intercourse etc. In these cases, therefore, Ignorance is a 'Natural Decisive Support, or 'Direct Inducement' (*pakati-upanissaya-paccaya*). It also may become an indirect inducement, by way of Object (*ārammanūpanissaya-paccaya*) of our thinking. This takes place, if, for example, someone remembers a former state of Ignorance combined with sensual enjoyment, and, in doing so, karmically unwholesome states spring up, such as sensual desire, grief, etc.

For the wholesome (*kusala*), Karma-formations, Ignorance can only be a condition by way of Decisive Support (*upanissaya*), never by way of Co-nascence (*saha-jāta*) etc., since wholesome consciousness at that very moment of course cannot be associated with any unwholesome phenomenon, such as

Ignorance. Ignorance is a 'National Decisive Support' or 'Direct Inducement' (*pakatupanissaya*), for example, if, induced by Ignorance and vanity, one exerts oneself to attain the absorptions, and thus finally, through perseverance, reaches these wholesome states of mind. Ignorance may also be for wholesome Karma-formations a 'Decisive Support' or 'Inducement by way of Object' (*ārammanūpanissaya*), if, for example, one reflects on Ignorance as the root of all misery in the world, and thus finally attains Insight, and entrance into one of the 4 supermundane paths of Holiness.

For Ignorance s. *avijja*; for Karma-formations s. *sankhāra*.

"Through the Karma-formations is conditioned Consciousness" (*sankhāra-paccayā viññāṇaṁ*). This proposition teaches that the wholesome and unholesome Karma-formations are the causes of future rebirth in an appropriate sphere (gati) the Karma-formations of the previous life condition the budding in a new mother's womb of a fresh psycho-physical aggregation of the 5 groups of existence (s. *khandha*), which here are represented by conciousness (*viññāṇa*). All such Karma resultant (*vipaka*) consciousness, however, as e.g. eye-consciousness (seeing) etc., as well as all the mental phenomena associated therewith (feeling, etc.) are karmically neutral. It should be understood that already from the very first moment of conception in the mother's womb, this karma-resultant consciousness of the embryonic being is functioning.

Against Dr. Paul Dahlke's misconception of the Paticcasamuppāda as 'one single karmical moment of personal experience', and of the 'simultaneity' of all the 12 links of this formula, I should like to state here distinctly that the interpretation of the P. given here as comprising 3 successive lives, not only agrees with all the different schools of Buddhism, and all the ancient commentaries, but also is fully identical with the explanations given already in the canonical Suttas. Thus, for example, it is said verbatim in Nidāna-Samyutta (S.XII, 51): "Once **Ignorance** (1) and Clinging (9) are extinguished, neither karmically meritorious, nor demeritorious, nor imperturbable **Karma-formations** (2=10) are produced, and thus no **Consciousness** (3=11) will spring up again in a new mother's womb". And further: "For, if consciousness were not to appear in the mother's womb, would in that case **Mentality and Corporeality** (4) arise?" Cf. above diagram.

The purpose of the Buddha in teaching the P. was to show to suffering mankind how, depending on Ignorance and Delusion, this present existence, and suffering has come about, and how through extinction of Ignorance, and of the Craving and Clinging conditioned thereby, no more rebirth will follow, and thus standstill of the process of existence will have been realized and therewith the extinction of all suffering.

"Through Consciousness conditioned are Corporeality and Mentality" (*viññāṇa-paccayā nāmarūpaṁ*). This proposition implies that without consciousness there can be no mental and physical process of existence. By Mentality (*nāma*) is here to be understood the karma-resultant (*vipāka*) mental phenomena, such as feeling (*vedanā*), perception (*saññā*), volition (*cetanā*: non-karmical volition is here meant), consciousness-impression (*phassa*), advertence (*manasikāra*) (M. 9, S. XII, 2). For the basic 7 mental phenomena inseparably associated with every state of consciousness, s. *nāma*. By Corporeality (*rūpa*) are meant the 4 physical elements (s. *dhātu*) and the corporeality dependent thereon (s. *khandha*, I).

Mentality is always conditioned through consciousness; i.e. Consciousness (*viññāṇa*) is for Mentality (*nāma*) a condition by way of Conascence (*sahajāta*), Mutuality (*aññamañña*), Association (*sampayutta*) etc., since the 4 mental groups at all times form an inseparable unit.

Consciousness (*viññāṇa*) is for Corporeality *(rūpa)* a condition by way of Co-nascence only at the moment of conception, thereafter a condition by way of Post-nascence *(pacchājāta-paccaya; paccaya* II) and Nutriment (*āharā*), i.e. as a support. Just as the repeatedly arising hunger is a condition and support for the pre-arisen body, so is the consciousness arising afterwards, a condition and support for the maintenance of this pre-arisen body.

"Through Mentality and Corporeality are conditioned the 6 Bases" (*nāma-rūpa paccayā saṭāyatanaṁ).* The 6 Bases are a name for the 5 physical sense-organs and, as 6th, the Mind-Base (*manāyatana*), i.e. consciousness.

Mentality (*nāma;* s. 3) is for the 5 physical Bases (*āyatana*), or sense-organs, a condition by way of Post-nascence. Cf. end of 3.

Mentality *(nāma),* i.e. feeling etc., is for the 6th Base, or consciousness—as being always inseparably associated therewith—a condition by way of Co-nascence etc.

Corporeality *(rūpa)* here the 4 elements, are for the 5 physical Bases *(ayatana),* or sense-organs, a condition by way of Support *(nissaya).*

Corporeality *(rūpa),* here the 5 physical sense-organs, are for the 6th Base *(āyatana)* i.e. consciousness, a condition by way of Support and

Pre-nascence *(purejāta-paccaya).*

"Through the 6 Bases is conditioned the (sensorial and mental) Impression" *(saṭāyatana-paccayā phasso),* for without the 5 physical Bases, or sense-organs, there can be no sense-impressions: and without the 6th Base, or consciousness, there can be no Mental Impression.

Thus, the 5 Physical Bases eye etc. are for the corresponding 5 sense-impressions (visual impression etc.) a condition by way of Support *(nissaya)* and Pre-nascence (*purejāta*), whereas the 6th, the Mind-Base (consciousness), is for the Mental Impression a condition by way of Co-nascence, Association, Mutuality etc.

"Through Impression is conditioned Feeling" *(phassa-paccayā vedanā),* i.e. the sensorial and the mental Impressions are for the Feeling associated therewith a condition by way of Co-nascence, Association, Mutuality etc.

"Through Feeling is conditioned Craving" *(vedanā-paccayā taṇhā).* Any (karma-resultant) Feeling, whether agreeable, disagreeable or neutral, bodily or mental, past or expected, may become for Craving a condition of Decisive Support by way of Object (*arammanupanissaya*). Even physically and mentally painful feeling may, through the desire to be released therefrom, become for craving a condition of Decisive Support by way of Object (*ārammaṇupanissaya*).

"Through Craving is conditioned Clinging" *(taṇhā-paccayā upaddnaṃ).* 'Clinging' is explained as an intensified form of 'Craving'. It is of 4 kinds: (1) Clinging to Sensuality, (2) to erroneous Views, (3) to Rules and Ritual, (4) to Personality-Belief. Sensuous Craving is to (1) a condition of Natural Decisive Support *(pakati-upanissaya).* For (2-4),

Craving is a condition by way of Co-nascence, Mutuality, Root *(hetu)* etc. It also may be a condition of Natural Decisive Support. For example, through Craving for heavenly rebirth etc. people often may be induced to cling to certain rules and rituals, with the hope of reaching thereby the object of their desires.

"Through Clinging is conditioned the Process of Becoming" (*upādāna-paccayā bhavo*), i.e. the wholesome and unwholesome active Karma-Process of Becoming *(kamma-bhava),* as well as the karma-resultant (*vipaka*) passive process, the so-called 'Rebirth-Process' (*upapatti-bhava*).

2. Dr. David Brazier:

The Nature of Buddhism

The Buddhist agenda is a change of heart for the world. The slogan that goes with this is "Inner peace, outer peace," or, we could say, inner transformation, outer transformation. Buddhism is looking to bring people to a transformation of consciousness—an arising of wisdom and compassion that knows no boundaries. This is a way of liberation, but not the kind of liberation that is commonly thought of.

The idea of liberation comes from pre-Buddhist India. The pre-Buddhist idea was to release the soul from the confines of this benighted world. Liberation meant that the soul might be free and so be able to return to god, leaving the world behind. The Buddha stood these ideas on their head. There is no soul of that kind, he said—no soul that could flee the world and make a refuge in a metaphysical realm. The real refuge for our lives is here, embodied in wise people, skilful practice and harmonious communities. These are what we need. He called them three jewels.

After he died, people tried to deify him and return to their old ways, but the message is still therefore those who have ears to hear. He did not want to be a god. The liberation that the Buddha speaks of is not the liberation of the soul from the world, but the act of liberating the world from our own greed, hate and delusion—the three poisons. When we can do that we will find that the paradise we yearn for is not far away.

The key to this is transformation: the transformation of three poisons into three jewels. We sometimes say inner transformation, but this makes Buddhism seem more inward looking than it actually is. People are not basically inward looking. People are engaged in a world. This is a real world. Reality is constantly knocking on our door. Just turning inward is not the answer. We will not bring about wise people, skilful action and harmonious communities by ignoring the knock on the door or saying "Nobody at home."

Transformation—the liberation of the world from graspingness, oppression and folly—means being willing to open the door in a hospitable and generous way. An inward transformation actually means a revisioning of the outside world. When we look at the stranger on our doorstep, do we see a friend-to-be or an alien presence? Do we make this world our friend or our enemy? If we make it our enemy, then we will surely be in the business of trying to find an individual salvation for our individual soul. That would certainly not be the Buddha's way.

The Buddha's way was simply to give his life to the service of the world. That service was the overcoming of the poisons of the mind by transforming them into love, compassion and wisdom.

This transformation both comes about by and is expressed in action. The Buddha walked. Wherever he went he made the minimum possible demand for his personal needs and gave the maximum he was capable of to help the local people to grow in wisdom, in skilful means and in compassionate community. He tended the sick, he taught, he mediated in disputes, he advocated for peace, he protected animals, he cultivated kindness, he helped people achieve wisdom, and he encouraged others to adopt a similar approach to life.

A Symbol of Transformation

Consider the lotus flower. This is a symbol of the kind of transformation the Buddha was interested in. The lotus is one of the most beautiful flowers in the world. It is stunningly lovely. It stands above the water with its magnificent petals wide open to the sun. Beads of water may splash onto the petals and seems only to enhance the beauty, sitting like little jewels sparkling in the light.

The lotus also bears fruit. Uncommonly among plants the fruit and flower are there simultaneously. The flowers do not fall until well after the fruit has formed.

Where does this wondrous plant draw its nourishment from? Whence comes its strength and beauty? We know, of course. It comes from the mud and slime down in the dark depths of the pond. This is the secret of the lotus, to transform what seems to us loathsome into what seem to us the epitome of fineness. This is the symbol of transformation.

The Buddhist approach, therefore, is like the lotus. We can imagine ourselves as a lotus plant. We have roots. Each of us has a history. Each of us was once a little person surrounded by powerful adults. The adults did not always do what we wanted them to do. They did not even always act as they should. Each of us has wounds. We have had struggles. We have had disasters and triumphs—things we feel smug about and things that make us cringe with shame. All of us have been oppressed in some degree at some time. Some more, some less, perhaps. We all have mud in which to grow our lotus.

The stem of the lotus symbolises spiritual training. If you are a Buddhist, this term has a particular connotation. But you might be a Christian or a Jew or a Muslim, or you might be of no particular named faith. Whatever, you are bound to have done some spiritual training of some sort. You have learnt some discipline. You have had some education. You have been drawn out and shaped, strengthened and skilled. You have acquired ways of understanding the things you have experienced in life and some of these ways have made you into a more wise and compassionate person. This training, whether systematic or just a product of circumstance, is the stem of the lotus.

Training starts at home with our parents, continues at school, goes on through higher education and career and adult relationships. All these are training of one sort or another. We are learning all the time. We learn skills and knowledge. We learn to cope with challenges and crises. We learn to be useful and to help others. Everybody has had some spiritual training. From the Buddhist perspective, the most important training is whatever enables us to let go of self-seeking ways and find a way of being that is constructive and creatively engaged. So of the training we have participated in life may have been counter-training. We may have learnt bad habits – cynicism, aggression, greed and addictions. There is pollution too in the lotus pond.

When we talk about spiritual training we are not talking about spirits, plural, as in ghosts. We are talking about spirit, as when we say that a person has a lot of spirit — a quality not an entity. It means courage, fortitude and flexibility. The stem of the lotus is strong and it bends. If it were stiff and brittle it would break. It can go with the flow, but not too far. It can bow with what is good and hold against what is not. It can sway with an impact, and come back again. Buddhism has a lot to say about spiritual training.

The roots and the stem support the flower. What are the petals on our lotus flower? They are all the good actions we perform in the world. I write books, I see clients for psychotherapy, I teach, I build friendship. How do I do these things? Behind them lies much learning, just as the flower depends upon the stem. It was hard work learning to write. It was a long training to became a psychotherapist—and more than that, it required a lot of life experience. It took the overcoming of many previous mistakes and mess-ups to make a good marriage. Flowers do not appear in the sky, they appears on strong stems that grow out of the earth.

It is very important to see our flowers. If we do not realise that we each are a flower, then we will not understand, why we are here nor why anything matter?

It is important to see our mud, but if mud is all we see, then we will just remain a dirty pool and no lotuses will grow. It is important to see the whole picture. There are those who want flowers without mud and there are those who see only mud and never produce flowers. This is, in both cases, because the stem is being overlooked. It is the stem that transforms mud into flowers and it is the stem that nourishes flowers from mud.

Layers of Mud

We have all encountered suffering, both that of ourselves and that of others. We have all evolved strategies for coming to terms with, overcoming or avoiding that suffering. We can pause a moment and notice the suffering that is in us still. It is close at hand or does it seem distant today? Everybody has internalised sufferings and oppressions. These things can build in the mind.

When we become conscious of the suffering we, carry, we may also start becoming conscious of the strategies that we use of keep that suffering within bounds. Perhaps we avoid some people. Perhaps we seek security in a variety of ways. Perhaps we have become a bit cynical. Perhaps we have became addicted to things we regard as comforts–tobacco, alcohol, television, sex, or whatever.

As we do so we may begin to feel uncomfortable. We do not like to think of ourselves as addicted, cynical, grasping or defensive, but, if we are honest, probably we are all of these things. Buddhism is not interested in sin, but it is interesed in honesty. If we are going to effect a transformation in life, we need to begin with a recognition of the state we are in. Honesty is a first step. The roots of the lotus need to be deep in the mud. So, first, find you mud.

When we look at our mud, we see that we do harm. There are strategies that we have evolved in order to cope with the sufferings that we have internalised and learnt to fear. These strategies do harm to others. In our effort to combat the oppressions we have experienced, we ourselves become oppressors.

This is the normal situation. It is a hard thing to face. Buddhist psychology begins, therefore, with an attempt to face suffering, to face what it brings up, and to have a square look at what we do with it.

Even those who are actively in combating oppressions in the world, may not have done this initial self-examination, or, if they have, may not have taken any action to do something about what they discovered. On the other hand there are an even greater number of people who, having become aware in some degree of their own suffering, have concluded that they have nothing much to offer.

The Stem of the Lotus

The message of hope that is the core of Buddhism is the idea that the mud itself can be transformed into lotus flowers. The implication is, on the one hand, that no matter what may lie in our history or what degree of mess we may have got our life into, there is always still the possibility of transforming that very mess into a resource — into nourishment for a lotus flower. On the other hand, there is also an implication that if we do not give attention to the stem of the lotus, the mud will stay mud and the flower will die.

The stem of the lotus is made by what, in Buddhism, is called cultivation. There is cultivation of body, and mentality.

Asked to described what this training is like, the Buddha said, suppose that a person decides to leave the conventional life behind and dedicate themselves completely to spiritual training, what will they do? Well, first he (or she) will attend to his own behaviour. He will attempt to clean up his act. He will make sure that he is not living in a way that is a direct cause of death and suffering to other living beings. He will liberate himself from the slavery of living for money. He will avoid getting caught in the complications and restrictions that new sexual involvement brings. He will pay particular attention to what he thinks and says, will avoid words that lead to conflict, disparagement of others, or the trivialising of life, and learn to speak words that make for peace, inspiration, compassion, and love, words that are wise and that touch the heart. Finally, he will work to eliminate compulsiveness. In particular, he will stop using alcohol and drugs, under the influence of which he is likely to lose his resolve and beacame involved in precisely the opposite behaviours from those listed here.

These will be her (or his) first concerns. If she tries to do this, she will encounter two difficulties. These are the habits or the senses and the habits of the mind. To overcome the first, it will be necessary to develop mindfulness. Mindfulness means keeping in mind the pupose of one's life. What we are talking about here is the way to make one's life. What we are talking about here is the way to make one's life meaningful. Many, perhaps most, people do not seriously undertake the task of making their life meaningful in anything more than a rather scattered and piecemeal fashion. Meaning is not given to life by the gods, it is created by the way we live. It is up to us to make it so.

A person following the Buddha's directions has confidence that she is creating a meaningful life my life a life—that they will be able to look back upon and think, "I did what I had to do—I made a meaningful life—my life was well lived." This was the Buddha's basic criterion. When we look back, are we going to be able to say that, or will we say, "I don't know where it all went," or "What was that all about then?" or, worse, "I wasted my time," or "The older I got the more bitter I became." When we are dying, the fortune we made will look trivial, the affairs we had will look inconsequential or harmful, the revenge we sought will be seen to have harmed ourselves certainly, and even if it succeeded in harming our enemy, the satisfaction in that will have paled.

Mindfulness means to know, in each moment of life, that this moment matters. If one can learn to live like that one will have a full and satisfying life. One will be alive. Inso far as we do not do so, although we look as though we are living, we will really be dead spiritually. Death is busy living most people's lives for them. The Buddha was not willing to let Death have his while he was still in it. So, mindfulness is the antidote to the habits of the senses—the habits that inveigle us into taking the extra care or avoiding the task we feel squeamish about. If we just live "looking after myself", the one day we will look back on a trivial and superficial existence. So much for the pitfalls of the habits of our senses.

The habits of the mind lie deeper. The mind is full of constructions that we have been building since infancy and perhaps before. These constructions can cause us trouble because generally we have our mind organised in a self-serving way. Most of what we have learnt in life, and virtually all of what we have made up, has been created to support our beliefs about who and what we are, how we think we should be treated and so. In other words, all our constructs revolve around self.

The Buddha, therefore, said that the person who wishes to create a meaningful life, will have to do something about the way his (or her) mind is. It is not so much that he will need to clean everything out of it as that he will need to start using whatever is therein a new way. He will need to take stock. To do so it will be necessary to study the mind. To study the mind he will need to learn stillness and silence and also skills in inward inquiry. The two main branches of Buddhist meditation method are called "stopping" and "looking".

He will learn to keep his attention in here and now and to observe what arises spontaneously. He will also learn to make searching inquiries into his own mentality and motives. Sometimes this will be unpleasant. Some of what he finds, there will be painful and some will be ugly. He is likely to feel contrition and even revulsion sometimes. He will come face to face with the emptiness of much of what he had previously devoted time and energy to.

This is what the Buddha said about growing the stem of the lotus. He also said that the person who does these things will, in the process, discovers bliss. She (or he) will find that the mind is not a monster and that the world is not evil. She will find that the constructions she had previously filled her mind with change. They are impermanent. She will realize that the things she used to put such store by are becoming burdensome to her and other things that she had previously feared or avoided are becoming more friendly. She will begin to feel deeply that the world that matters is this world, not a set of fantasies. She will no longer be in pusuit of the perfection of self, but will feel drawn to the needs of the "not-self", the real world. In this transformation she will experience a great liberation and exhilaration that seems to well up spontaneously from the roots of her being. She will be energized as never before.

The Lotus Flower

The stem does not really exist for its own sake. It exists in order to effect the transformation. It grows up through the dark toward the sunshine. Then, it breaks the surface into a new bright world and unfolds into a beautiful flower. Having become a flower, it does not stop growing. It goes on to produce many fruits. The Buddha, after his enlightenment, kept on developing. Ever new ways of presenting the teachings flowed from him. He learnt things as the number of followers increased. The sangha took shape, and new precedents were set for how they should live and what they should do. This process was continuous. Eventually the Buddha died. By then the seeds were scattered all over India and soon they spread further afield. Very few individuals have had such an extensive effect upon the people of this planet.

One person can make a lot of difference. This depends, however, upon the lotus flowering. Some seeds just stick in the mud. Some grow but do not break the surface and so remain in the dark. Some continue upward. This depends upon a kind of faith. It is not faith in something supernatural. It is faith in life. Death will come eventually, of course. But while alive, live. There are encounters like this between the Buddha and Death in the Buddhist texts. Death comes and tempts him. Death says, why not just opt for an easy life—you are famous now—why not cash in on your reputation? Or, on another occasion—why not just come to me now—wouldn't it be easier? The Buddha replies to this last—you will have your time but for now I have important things to do. There is a story that after the Buddha's enlightenment, Death stalked him for seven years trying to find a chink to get in by. At the end of seven years, the text paints a picture of Death sitting down looking totally disconsolate. He say, “For seven years I have pursued the Buddha at every step; but he was always alert and I did not have a chance. I have been like a crow that come down thinking to have found a tender delicacy that turns out to be a stone. The crow flies away again. I too have given up.”

The lotus flower rises above the water—above the darkness of death-in-life. Buddhist training brings us to this point and enables us to give this life to others. In the same text as the story of Death as a disappointed crow, there is the Buddha full of enthusiasm still, saying, “From land to land, I shall go, training disciples far and wide.” All this is in the Sutta Nipata.

So, the flower is the deathless state but the purpose of the flower is the fruit and the fruit is service to others. A Buddha has much to do when there is a whole pond to be filled with lotus flowers. When we look around, there is much suffering in the world. Some suffering is of the unavoidable kind. There are earthquakes and storms. There are the challenges in life that help to bring us to maturity. There is another kind, however. This is the death-in-life variety that we could call defeat of the spirit. It is this latter that Buddhism exists to combat.

Whether we call Buddhism a religion or not is simply a matter of definition. Religions as we know them had hardly been invented when the Buddha lived. It was really king Ashoka who made Buddhism into what we recognize as a religion. Primitive Buddhism was a call to a life of deathlessness (the flower) and service (the fruit).

3. JHĀNA, ‘Absorption’ (trance, meditation) refers chiefly to the four meditative Absorptions of the Fine-material Sphere (*rūpa-jjhāna* or *rūpāvacarajjhāna;* s. *avacara*). They are achieved through the attainment of Full (or Attainment -, or Ecstatic) Concentration (*appanā*, s. *samādhi*), during which there is a complete, though temporary, suspension of fivefold sense-activity and of the 5 Hindrances (s. *nivaraṇa*). The state of consciousness, however, is one of full alertness and lucidity. This high degree of concentration is generally developed by the practice of one of the 40 subjects of Tranquillity Meditation (*samatha-kammaṭṭhdna;* s. *bhāvanā*).—Often also the 4 Immaterial spheres (*arūpāyatana*) are called Absorptions of the Immaterial Sphere (*arūpa-jjhāna* or *arūpāvacarajjhāna*). The stereotype text, often met with in the Suttas, runs as follows:

(1) "Detached from sensual objects, O monks, detached from unwholesome states of mind, the monk enters into the first absorption, which is accompanied by Thought-Conception *(vitakka)* and Discursive Thinking (*vicāra*), is born of Detachment (= Concentration: *samādhi)* and filled with Rapture (*piti*) and Joy (*sukha*).

(2) "After the subsiding of thought-conception and discursive thinking, and by gaining inner tranquillity and oneness of mind, he enters into a state free from thought-conception and discursive thinking, the second absorption, which is born of Concentration (*samādhi*), and filled with Rapture (*piti*) and Joy (*sukha*).

(3) "After the fading away of rapture, he dwells in equanimity, mindful, clearly conscious; and he experiences in his person that feeling of which the Noble Ones say, 'Happy lives the man of equanimity and attentive mind'; thus he enters the 3rd absorption.

(4) "After having given up pleasure and pain, and through the disappearance of previous joy and grief,

he enters into a state beyond pleasure and pain, into the 4th absorption, which is purified by Equanimity *(upekkhā)* and mindfulness.

(5) "Through the total overcoming of the perceptions of matter, however, and through the vanishing of sense-reactions and the non-attention to the perceptions of variety, with the idea, 'Boundless is space', he reaches the Sphere of Boundless Space (*ākāsānañcāyatana*) and abides therein.

"By 'perceptions of matter' (*rūpa-saññā*) are meant the absorptions of the fine-material sphere, as well as those objects themselves..." (Vis X, 1).

"By 'perceptions of sense-reactions' (*patigha-saññā*) are meant those perceptions that have arisen due to the impact of sense-organs (eye etc.) and the sense-objects (visible objects etc.). They are a name for the perception of visible objects etc., as it is said (Jhāna-Vibh.): What are here the perceptions of sense-reactions? They are the perceptions of visible objects, sounds, etc.'—'Surely, they do no longer exist even for one who has entered the 1st absorption etc., for at such a time the Five-sense consciousness is no longer functioning. Nevertheless, this is to be understood as having been said in praise of this immaterial absorption, in order to incite the striving for it" (Vis X, 16).

"Perceptions of variety *(nānatia-saññā)* are the perceptions that arise in various fields, or the various perceptions" (ib). Hereby, according to Vis. X, 20, are meant the multiform perceptions outside the absorptions.

(6) "Through the total overcoming of the Sphere of boundless Space, and with the idea 'Boundless is consciousness', he reaches the Sphere of Boundless

Consciousness (*viññāṇañcāyatana*) and abides therein.

(7) "Through the total overcoming of the Sphere of Boundless Consciousness, and with the idea: 'Nothing is there', he reaches the Sphere of Nothingness (*ākiñcaññāyatana*) and abides therein.

(8) "Through the total overcoming of the sphere of Nothingness he reaches the Sphere of Neither-Perception-nor-Non-Perception (*nevasaññā-n'āsaññā-yatana*) and abides therein".—

"Thus the 1st absorption is free from 5 things (i.e. the Hindrances, *nivaraṇa,* q.v.), and 5 things are present (i.e. the Factors of Absorption, (*jhān' anga*). Whenever the monk 'enters the 1st absorption, there have vanished: Sensuous Desire, Ill-will, Torpor and Sloth, Restlessness and Scruples, Doubts; and there are present: Thought-Conception (*vitakka*). Discursive Thinking *(vicāra),* Rapture *(piti),* Joy *(sukha),* and Concentration *(samādhi).* In the 2nd absorption there are present: Rapture, Joy and Concentration; in the 3rd: Joy and Concentration: in the 4th: Equanimity (*upekkhā*) and Concentration" (Vis. IV).

The 4 absorptions of the Immaterial Sphere (s. above 5-8) still belong, properly speaking, to the 4th absorption as they possess the same two constituents. The 4th fine-material absorption is also the base or starting point (*pādaka-jhāna* q.v.) for the attaining of the Higher Spiritual Powers *(abhñiāa,* q.v.).

In the Abhidhamma, generally a fivefold, in stead of a fourfold division of the fine-material absorptions is used: the 2nd absorption has still the constituent 'Discursive Thinking' (but without Thought-Conception), while the 3rd, 4th and 5th correspond to the 2nd, 3rd and 4th, respectively, of the fourfold division (s. Tab. I, 9-13). This fivefold division is based on Sutta texts like A. VIII, 63.

For the 8 absorptions as objects for the development of insight *(vipassanā)*, see *samatha-vipassanā*.—Full details in Vis. VIII-X.

7

The Art, Relics, Sculpture and Archaeology

As a definition, Relic is 1, part of holy person's body or belongings kept after his death as object of reverence; momento, souvenir; (pl) dead body, remains, of person, 2 (pl) what has survived destruction or wasting, remnant, residue, scraps; (sing) surviving trace or memorial of custom, period, people, etc. object interest for its age or associations.

and

Sculpture, an art of forming representations of objects etc. or abstract designs in the round or in relief by chiselling stone, curving wood, or similar process: work of sculpture.

and

Archaeology, study of ancient culture through their material remains, remembrance matter of history.

All the above subjects are highly relevant and significantly important to know the high standard of Buddhist Culture in India and elsewhere.

During the reign of emperor Ashoka, he employed various symbol and means to proclaim the religious doctrine of Buddhism. Among the Buddhists Sakyamuni Buddha is not worshipped in physical form but it symbolizes in various ways. The depiction of the Ashokan pillars and traditional Yaksha images is the clear example of Buddhist culture of this period.

The most significant development of Buddhist

culture of these elements took place in the Kushan (Scythian) King's period spreaded between (1st century B C to 3rd century A D). It was here in Gandhara the human figure of Buddha was first sculpted in stone.

In Gandhara region (Kabul, Swat) there are some monasteries in stone. Images of standing or seated Buddha in Taxila and Jalalabad region have strong Hellenistic influences. The two colossal rock-cut superb images of Buddha existed at Bamiyan which was destroyed by Taliban, Muslim fundamentalist, radical groups but they had to flee away when moderate groups took over reign from them. The museum at Taxila has an extraordinary collection of coins and superb examples of Gandharan art – finely curved images of Buddha and the Bodhisattuas. The museum of Lahore also has a priceless collection of Gandharan art.

India there are over 700 museums, where there are some Gandharan collections. But there is no centre of Sakyan (Scythian) Indian Buddhist geneological museum where people can see their story.

The learning of Buddhist scripture making was a part of education in Buddhist centre of learning at Nalanda and Vikramsila. Therefore, Buddhist culture received a high excellence. A Chinese pilgrim recorded that when he visited the University of Nalanda he found a great statue of Avoloreitesvara and a picture of Maitreya Buddha. There are now numerous images of Buddha which are made in different countries in secterial line of Therovada and Mahayana, (The lesser and the greater vehicle) In the Therovada, Buddha was considered as a historic figure, whereas in the Mahayana, there are numerous symbols representing Sakyamuni or

Bodhisattva. The tantric Buddhism which represent Shakti (female deities) has been figures in many ways to get a perfect idea of the spirit of tantra. The Ajanta frescoes were painted between 2nd century B C and 1st half of 6th century A D.

The revered Sachi Stupa in India and Shwedagon Pagoda where Buddha's relics are enshrined.

A Buddhist stupa shaped in two ways (designs): (1) Tower shaped, (2) Dome shaped.

One of the Buddha's Collar-bones, holy relics was deposited in the stupa on the top of Missaka hills (Chetiya) and the famous tooth of Buddha kept at Dantapura in Sri Lanka.

In Arakan, Andaw Pagoda (Stupa) was build in 1531- 33 where the tooth relic of Sakyamuni is enshrined.

There is a story Kesa Dhatu (hair relics) of Sakyamuni. During the seventh week after enlightenment, Sakyamuni was meditating under a tree called rajayatana tree. On the 50th morning, after his long fast for seven weeks, two merchants came to his presence. They were called Tapussa and Bhallika. In fact, they were going in a different direction to another city. Tapussa and Bhallika offered the Buddha rice cakes and honey.

The two merchants by taking two refuges—in the Buddha and the Dhamma became the first lay followers of the Sakyamuni Buddha. There was no Sangha or order of monks then. They requested Buddha for something sacred to keep with them. The Buddha wiped his head with his right hand and got some hair and gave those to them. This hair was called Kesa Dhatu (hair relics), which was preserved during Sakyamuni's existential life.

Buddha has been represented in Buddhist culture

in many forms (Mudra):

1. The Maitreya Buddha (the future Buddha), embodiment of all Buddha's loving kindness and compassion. According to some believe (faith) a Buddha only appears in the world when the teaching of a previous Buddha have been lost and when beings will be receptive to his message.

2. Sakyamuni Buddha (historical Buddha) is seated on a lotus throne symbolizing the seat of enlightenment and purity.

3. Amitava Buddha (Amida): the Buddha of infinite light (wisdom).

The Birth in Lumbini Park

The queen Mahamaya left Kapilavastu the capital of Sakya Kingdom for the capital of her father's kingdom (Koliya country). On the way, she rested in the garden called Lumbini Park. While she rested underneath one of the Sala trees, her baby boy Siddhartha was born. It was an auspicious day, the birth took place on a full moon day in the year 623 B C. After the birth of her son, the Queen Mahamaya immediately returned to Kapilavastu, which is now at Tilaurakot in Nepal. The Sakyans and the Koliyas were neighbours separated by the river Rohini. Lumbini has been declared as world heritage centre by UNESCO in the year 1997.

According to some Buddhist literature, Kapilavastu was situated on the river, which was called Bhagirathi. It was common term to identify all rivers in the area Bhagirathi's (Bless river) that finally unite with holy Ganges or the Ganga. We can still see the remnants of a moat and walls at the site of Tilaurakat the walls are 10 ft wide. Unless it was a capital city, it could not have had walls. The area of Kapilavastu is around 1700 ft by 1300 ft.

It was too huge for monastic complex.

The Lumbini Park is about 24 miles north-east of Kapilavastu. It is marked by king Ashoka's inscription at Lumbini. Ashoka erected one of his commemorative pillars here. Chinese traveller Hiuen-Tsang visited the site. It has been declared as world heritage centre by the UNESCO in the year 1997.

From Kapilavastu Gautama Buddha went through the places to see the truth: Vaishali, Sravasti and then to Bodhgaya (Uruvela) on the bank of the river Niranjana, where he attained enlightenment.

Bodhgaya: Place of Enlightenment – Buddhahood

Six years of retreat across the river Niranjana about 1 mile from the place of enlightenment, there is a high mount overgrowth with trees and shrubs. It was the site of Sujata's home (Village Urubella). Sujata offered cooked sweet-milked rice to the ascetic Gautama. In the evening after the meal he went to Gaya and looked for a suitable place devoting to meditation under the Bodhi tree with his face to the east and attained enlightenment and Buddhahood.

Buddhahood

When Buddha attained enlightenment under the Bodhi tree at Bodhgaya, six colour of the Halo emanated from his body. The colours were blue from his hair, golden yellow from the flesh and blood, white from the bones and teeth and scarlet from the palms, heel and lips as they became blended together a six composite colour was formed which latter adopted as the world 'Buddhist flag'.

The First Watch (6:00 P.M.– 0:00 P.M.). He attained the power of racing up the past of his own life. It is understood that a Buddha attained normal power of mind/memory, which could perceive itself his own cyclic existence.

The Middle Watch (10:00 P.M.–2:00 P.M.). Analysis of Karma; Dharma four noble truth: 1. The truth of suffering, 2. The truth of the cause of suffering, 3. The truth of the cessations of suffering, and 4. The truth of the noble path that leads to the cessations of suffering.

The Last Watch (2:00 A.M.–4:00 A.M.). He got the power of understanding the cause of all evil and how to get rid of them.

The 32 bodily marks of a great man are as follows:

1. He has feet with a level tread.
2. On the soles of his feet wheels appear with a thousand spokes, with rims and hubs, in every way complete.
3. He has projecting heels.
4. He has long fingers.
5. He has soft and tender hands and feet.
6. He has fingers and toes evenly spread.
7. His ankles are over the exact middle of the tread.
8. His legs are sharply like those of antelopes.
9. While standing without stooping he can touch and rub his knees with both hands at once.
10. His privites are within sheath.
11. He has a golden complexion.
12. The texture of his skin is that no dust or dirt can lodge on it.
13. His body hair grows singly one only in each pore.
14. Each hair is straight, blue, black and curling to the right at its tip.

15. His body frame is straight.
16. His body has seven convex surfaces.
17. The upper part of his body is well built like that of a lion.
18. He has no hello between his shoulder blades.
19. He has the symmetrical projection of a banyan tree, his stretch being the same as his height.
20. The curve of his shoulders is symmetrical.
21. He has an exquisite, actually sensitive sense of taste.
22. His jaws are like those of a lion.
23. He has forty teeth.
24. He has even teeth.
25. There are interstices between his teeth.
26. His teeth are sparking white.
27. His tongue is long and flexible.
28. His voice is like that of the Brahma and mellifluous like that Karravika bird's.
29. His eyes are intensely blue.
30. His eyelashes are long and sharply like those of a cow.
31. Between his eyebrows grows soft white hair like cotton-down.
32. His head is shapely like a royal turban.

Deer Park: Saranath

All the 50th day the Buddha thought of meeting his five friends, (Kondana, Bhaddya, Wappa, Mahanama and Assagi) in the Deer Park at Saranath—where Buddha delivered his first sermon to his sangha (group) and introduced the world of his doctrine of Ahimsa (non-violence). His proclamation of dhamma—the four fundamental truths, namely—(i) the sorrow (dukkha) exist, (ii) that has a cause (samudaya), (iii) that can be eliminated (nirodha) and (iv) that the way to accomplish this is to follow the eight fold ways (merga) which king Bhimbisara was imprisoned by his own son till the last days of his life. The Bhimbisara's jail is still in existence as an archaeological site at Rajgir. After the death of Gautama Buddha three convocations were held and the first was held at Rajagraha (in a cave temple) composed of 500 Mahatheras and presided over by the Ven. Mahakassapa, four months after the death of Buddha. The third Buddhist conference after the death of Gautama Buddha was held at Pataliputra (modern Patna) with the assistance of king Ashoka, 200 years after the death of Buddha which was attended by 1000 Mahatheras, headed by Ven. Moggalputtatissa.

Nalanda

Gautama Buddha stayed one time near Nalanda (later the site of a famous Buddhist university the ruins of which can still be seen). Here, a prominent follower of Mahavira (founder of Jain sect) crossed over to the religious group of Gautama Buddha and the ranks of his followers. In ancient India there was another Buddhist University of Vallabhi (7th and 8th century A D) in Kathiawara in UP. It was an important centre for Buddhist studies. Just as Nalanda specialised in Mahayana studies so the University of Vallabhi was the rival centre of Hinayana studies.

Sravasti

The capital of ancient kingdom Kosala of King Prasenjit. As a matter of fact it has been identified by Gen. Cunningham with the ruins Sahed – Mahed on the river Rapti, Irrabati, at present in Uttar Pradesh. Archaeologists found out archaic remnants of buildings and stupas of the Maurya period and not prior to this. In a way, an archaic sketch of the buildings of Jetavana where Gautama Buddha spent 24 rainy seasons, some holy relics (feretory) and a huge Buddha statue, which was built by king Prasenjit, were found here by the archaeologists.

Chinese traveller Hiuen-Tsang visited this site. In the Buddhist scripture, it is mentioned Gautama Buddha gave an exercise to Kisa Gautami to plunger her back into the existential when she overwhelmed with sorrow at the death of her child and prayed to restore the life of the child to Buddha. The famous wealthiest person of that time Anatha-Pindika belonged to this place.

Kusinara

Buddha attained Mahaparinivanna on the full moon day of the month Vesakha (April-May) 483 B C. Buddha told his disciples let not the honours due to my body trouble you, Ananda. This place was identified by Cunningham with Kasia in the Gorakhpur district now in Uttar Pradesh. There is no emphasis on the relic worship or various ceremonial forms of rituals. But, the worship of the tooth relic is given more prominence as facultative by some sects in both Hinayana and Mahayana Buddhism.

Notes

1. In Dhigha Nikaya it mentions – all who are on a pilgrimage to shrines, if they should die with devotion in their hearts during the course of their pilgrimage will be born – a good celestial realm there are four shrines (places), namely:

1. Lumbini = birth place

2. Bodh gaya = place of enlightenment
3. Saranath = first place of sermon
4. Kushinara = maha parinirbana

2. The Buddha who appears in every place any time and in all beings; also called by various other names such as Virocona Buddha, Amitabha Buddha, Dharmakaya Buddha, Pratyakka (Pachek Buddha) that which is. There are two forms—(1) they live in forest in seclusion, (2) live in human being but refrain from giving discourses. Gautama Buddha was Sammasam Buddha (the purified, the truly compassionate, the enlightened).

Sarabath is just 10 kms north of Varanasi in Uttar Pradesh, where Gautama Buddha delivered Dhamma Chakra. At the holy site emperor Ashoka erected the pillar on to of which the four lions formed the capital. The four lions seated back to back and their snarling (smiling) faces gaze toward the cardinal directions – North, South, East and West – that they protect. Below is a band with four wheels separated by fine renditions of four animals. The emblem of the wheel signifies the law of dhamma of spiritual progress (surely not merely material progress). The Dharma Chakra is a potent Buddhist symbol because it signifies the historic importance of Saranath.

Separating the four wheels are symbolic attributes that each devotee should acquire: the patient devotion of the majestic bull, the trustworthy strength and wisdom of the elephant, the ever — fearless vigilant power of the lion, and the swiftness and grace of the horse. The Dharma Chakra, the bull, an elephant, a lion and a horse-symbols of duty, wisdom, devotion, strength, vigilance and speed – were chosen as the seal of the Indian republic.

Ajanta: Rock-cut Buddhist caves situated about 100 kms north-east of Aurangabad containing world famous mural paintings illustrating scenes from the life of Buddha and also Jataka stories.

Amaravati: Buddhist Centre in the Guntur District, Andhra Pradesh right on the bank of the Krishna. The site now lies in ruins.

Lumbini: Birth place of Buddha, modern Rummidei in the district of Bhairhwa, Nepal, Tarai.

It has been noted, that the best paintings of the ancient India is the Buddhist paintings; that the sculpture of the golden days of the ancient Indian culture is the Buddhist sculpture that the earliest historical sculpture of India is also the Buddhist sculpture. The earliest historical inscription of India are the Buddhist inscriptions.

Gautama Buddha's presence is indicated by means of various symbols. The Gandhara images of the Buddha and the Bodhisattva began to make their appearance from about the middle of the 1st century B C and the Mathura images some time later. The noble quality of Buddha is represented as under:

Yellow : For holiness

White : For purity

Blue : For confidence

Red : For wisdom

Orange : For desirelessness

The mixed colour of all these represent higher degree of purity of mind and body.

Gautama Buddha delivered the eternal law (wheel of Dharma) his first sermon to five ascetics in the Deer Park (now in UP). It is called noble path between two extremes of self-indulgence and self-mortification – a Buddhist way of life.

8

The Art of Central Asia[1]

Central Asia with its eclectic outlook took over and recasted with considerable success the art forms of the great sedentary civilizations, those of the semi-classical of the East, of Iran, of Indo-Greek and Indo-Scythian art, of China and of Gupta India. The borrowing results are traceable in the cultural evolution of different zones, no doubt varying in their extent and intensity and extending from minute details to essential concepts of art style and iconography. The Iranian elements, however, predominate in the western zone, while south of the desert the Indian influence or traits have an upper hand along with the intruding Persian influence. The eastern zone has certainly close Chinese impact. Despite these diversities, the Central Asian peoples were close to each other in their spiritual outlook and artistic expression, with extraordinary analogies of style and iconography. The inexhaustible subject matter was provided by the Buddhist legends—the Jatakas—for the artists to display their talents. When elements from the Indian complex mythology, with the rich possibilities offered by Hindu and Tantric importations, were added, the scope of the artist was immensely extended. The vast material collected by the explorers and excavators from different nationalities no doubt reveals a bewildering diversity of style and treatment. This was due to the complex social and political conditions prevailing in the zones of artistic activities. The change of political powers during the long course of Central Asian history, passing on from one race to another differing in ideals and traditions in art and varying in psychological conception, was responsible for this lack of uniformity except on a religious plane.

Reference

1. The art of Central Asia is located at several centres on the northern and southern silk trade routes. The peoples in these regions took over the art forms of the great sedentary civilizations around them: those of the semi-classical cultures of the East, of Iran, of Indo-Greek and Indo-Scythians, of China, and of Gupta India. The borrowings, no doubt, vary in extent and intensity from minute reminiscences of detail to essential concepts of style and iconography. The Iranian element predominates in the western region, while the Chinese influence in the figurative arts is prominent in the eastern area of Central Asia nearer to or forming part of the Tang empire. The Indian influence associated with Buddhism and Gupta art made itself felt in Khotan and other places, varying, of course, in degree and dimension. Stylistic currents emanating from Central Asia itself are supposed to be instrumental not only in shaping Indo-Iranian trends of North-west India and Afghanistan, considered the southernmost offshoot of Central Asian art. They also reacted on the artistic evolution of Kashmir, on much of the ancient art of Tibet (particularly painting) and even on Chinese Buddhist painting (Bussagli: *op. cit.* p. 16-17). Several scholars have made a general study of Central Asian Art—sculptures and paintings, as also of specific areas. These include: Bussali, Mario: *Painting of Central Asia*—translated from the Italian by Lothian Small, Geneva, 1963; Talbot Rice, Tamara: *Ancient Arts of Central Asia,* London, 1965; Montebello, Phillippe de: *Along the Ancient Silk Routes—Central Asian Art from the West Berlin State Museums,* New York, 1982; Rowland, B: *The Wall Paintings of India, Central Asia and Ceylon,* Boston, Mass. 1938; F.H. Andrews: *Wall-Paintings from Ancient Shrines in Central Asia recovered by Sir Aurel Stein,* London, 1948; Nobuo Kumagai: *Central Asian Painting,* Tokyo; Gray, B: *Buddhist Cave Paintings at Tun huang,* London, 1959; Hackin, J.: *Buddhist Art in Central Asia,* London, 1936. For a comprehensive bibliography on Central Asian art, see Hambi's Article on the subject in the *Encyclopaedia of World* 99*Art,* Vol. I , pp. 837-38.

9
Questions on Sakya

Question: Is there any mention of Sakya tribe in Tibetan instory? If yes, was there any link with the Sakya clan in which Gautama Buddha was born?

Answer: In the 6th century B C the Sakya tribe was a small tribe living in the southern part of present-day Nepal. Sakya is a Sanskrit name and is mentioned in Tibetan history as the name of the tribe in which Siddhartha Gautama was born. The Sakya tribe had no role in Tibetan history. In the 6th century B C almost nothing was known of Tibet. (In those early centuries Nepal and Tibet did not exist as territorial entities by themselves.) Tibetan history begins with the closing decades of the 6th century A D: about A D 580 there is mention of a small principality which was later ruled by the celebrated Srong-brtsansgam-po (born 617, reign 630-49) whose father was grandfather were local rulers of that principality. By then the Sakya tribe of Siddhartha Gautama had been forgotten. In Tibetan history, therefore, there is no mention of the Sakya tribe of the 6th century B C except as Siddhartha Gautama's tribe. Of the time when the Sakya tribe flourished, there are no Tibetan historical records or other writings.

The name Sakya, however, occurs in Tibetan history. There is a Tibetan word spelt Sa-skya, pronounced Sakya. This is the name of a place in Tibet, where a monastery was founded in 1073. After the name of this place a Tibetan Buddhist school founded by Khon Konchog Gyalpo (1034-1102) took its name. This school and its head lama have been highly regarded in Tibet.

There is no link between Siddhartha Gautama's Sakya tribe of the 6th century B C with Sa-skya of Tibet, which became the centre of the Sa-skya school, called in Tibetan Sa-skya-pa, pronounced Sakyapa.

question: King Prasenjit's son was hostile to the Sakya clan. He massacred the Sakya clan when he became king. Was the place of massacre in India or in Nepal? Where was the exact location?

Answer: The Sakya tribe of Siddhartha Gautama was massacred by the King of Kosala, who was an ally of the King of Magadha. The King of Magadha, however, was a follower of the Buddha, as Siddhartha Gautama became known in history. Bimbisara and Ajatasatru were converted by the Buddha. (Incidentally, they were founders of the greatness of Magadha.) To the north, there was the Vrijji confederation, including the Licchavi clan. In the contest, finally Magadha came out victorious.

The Buddha was much distressed during his last years by the tact that his tribe, the Sakya, had been destroyed in the struggle for power. When the Buddha came to Kusinagara, also known as Kusinara, he heard of the massacre of his tribe. Although much concerned, the Buddha contemplated no steps in response.

It appears that the Sakya tribe remained in Kapilavastu. However, the territory of this rather small tribal state included the present-day district of Gorakhpur in northern UP. It would seem that the destruction of the Sakya tribe must have taken place in areas which are now partly in Nepal and partly in India. Perhaps the exact location cannot be pinpointed with any degree of certainty.

To the east of the Sakya tribal area was Videha,

one of the leading states of that time. Kosala (in Awadh, with the capital at Ayodhya) was ruled by Mahakosala, whose son was Prasenajit. He extended his kingdom to absorb the Sakya territory.

In Indian history, we read of a son of Prasenajit, who destroyed the Sakya tribe. In view of his defeat by Ajatasatru of Magadha, this son of Prasenajit was probably no more than a local ruler. We do not even know his name.

Question: How did the Lotus Sutra originate? What is its link with a Pali text?

Answer: It is believed that the *Lotus Sutra* was preached by the Buddha from his year 72 to his death at the age of 80, that is, during the last eight years of his life. The Buddha delivered all his teaching in Magadhi, which later became known as Pali. However, no Pali text of the *Lotus Sutra* has been discovered so far.

The Buddha says in the *Lotus Sutra* that this was his last and highest teaching and that it superseded everything that he taught after achieving Enlightenment up to his age of 72. It is said that the Buddha had all along been preparing his audiences for his final teaching, which was eventually given in the *Lotus Sutra.*

In no other sutra does the Buddha say that his final teaching was contained or would be embodied in the *Lotus Sutra.*

At several places in the *Lotus Sutra,* the Buddha uses phrases like Hinayana, Mahayana, Ekayana, Buddhayana, etc.

It is possible that when the Buddha was appropriated by the followers of Brahmanism (later called Hinduism) as an avatara of Vishnu, some inventive and imaginative mind(s) composed the

Lotus Sutra and passed it off as the Buddha's last major discourse. It is indeed curious that there is no Pali text of the *Lotus Sutra* although it is acknowledged on all hands that the Buddha preached in Magadhi.

In fact, a distinction has come to be made between Pali Buddhism and Sanskrit Buddhism. Sanskrit translation of several of the Buddha's teachings must have been made after the Buddha was ensconced in the Hindu pantheon as one more god. It is a moot point whether all teachings of the Buddha can be restored to their original text in Magadhi. We do know when those Sanskrit translations were made.

To sum up, we should take note of the following facts. (a) The earliest known collections of Buddhist texts, which became the basis of the Tripitakas of Southern Buddhism, did not include the *Lotus Sutra.* (b) The earliest Chinese translation of the *Lotus Sutra,* made in the 3rd century A D, followed a Sanskrit text. (c) The earliest known Sanskrit text of the *Lotus Sutra* dates from the 7 century AD. (d) The classification of the Buddha's teaching into Hinayana and Mahayana was not made during his lifetime but in the Buddhist Council held by Kaniska (78-101) in the 1st century A D, more than 500 years after the death of the Buddha (c. 483 B C).

Available evidence leads us to question the authenticity of the *Lotus Sutra* as a genuine teaching of the Buddha.

Perhaps it is not entirely fortuitous that the *Lotus Sutra* has not had a large following in India at any time in the 25 centuries since the death of the Buddha or that it achieved a significant status as a Buddhist text only in some countries of Northern Buddhism.

Question: How did the Lotus Sutra originate? What is its link with a Pali text?

Answer: It is believed that the *Lotus Sutra* was preached by the Buddha from his year 72 to the death at the age of 80, that is, during the last eight years of his life. The Buddha delivered all his teaching in Magadhi, which later became known as Pali. However, no Pali text of the *Lotus Sutra* has been discovered so far.

The Buddha says in the *Lotus Sutra* that this was his last and highest teaching and that it superseded everything that he taught after achieving Enlightenment up to his age of 72. It is said that the Buddha had all along been preparing his audiences for his final teaching, which was eventually given in the *Lotus Sutra.*

In no other sutra does the Buddha say that his final teaching was contained or would be embodied in the *Lotus Sutra.*

At several places in the *Lotus Sutra,* the Buddha uses phrases like Hinayana, Mahayana, Ekayana, Buddhayana, etc.

It is possible that when the Buddha was appropriated by the followers of Brahmanism (later called Hinduism) as an *avatara* of Vishnu, some inventive and imaginative mind(s) composed the *Lotus Sutra* and passed it off as the Buddha's last major discourse. It is indeed curious that there is no Pali text of the *Lotus Sutra* although it is acknowledged on all hands that the Buddha preached in Magadhi.

In fact, a distinction has come to be made between Pali Buddhism and Sanskrit Buddhism. Sanskrit translation of several of the Buddha's teachings must have been made after the Buddha was ensconced in the Hindu pantheon as one more god. It is a moot point whether all teachings of the Buddha can be restored to their original text in Magadhi. We do know when those Sanskrit translations were made.

To sum up, we should take note of the following facts. (a) The earliest known collections of Buddhist texts, which became the basis of the Tripitakas of Southern Buddhism, did not include the *Lotus Sutra.* (b) The earliest Chinese translation of the *Lotus Sutra,* made in the 3rd century A D, followed a Sanskrit text (c) The earliest known Sanskrit text of the *Lotus Sutra* dates from the 7th century A.D. (d) The classification of the Buddha's teaching into Hinayana and Mahayana was not made during his lifetime but in the Buddhist Council held by Kaniska (78-101) in the 1st century A D, more than 500 years after the death of the Buddha (c. 483 B C).

Available evidence leads us to question the authenticity of the *Lotus Sutra* as a genuine teaching of the Buddha.

Perhaps it is not entirely fortuitous that the *Lotus Sutra* has not had a large following in India at any time in the 25 centuries since the death of the Buddha or that it achieved a significant status as a Buddhist text only in some countries of Northern Buddhism.

10
Deoxyribonuclic Acid (DNA)

Since the ancient time, Sakyans were not remained confined to a small geographical area. They were divided into many nationalities. Many of them must have died out, but the progenation of Sakyan race is still alive. The analytical study on it could be two approaches. The first approach to bring into focus on history, anthropology, culture and other relevant stream of knowledge. The second approach on genealogical study, which might show some evidences.

According to geneticist, gene may influence personality dramatically by nature. It might play an influential role in personality tracts mores and types of characteristics like passivity, independency, hostilities etc. This is the other aspect of Genetic Study which is called Behavioural Sciences (Study).

During my visit to London (July 1999), when I brought up in question to Dr. Mark G. Thomas, a research geneticist University College, London; does the centre have interest in the subject of Sakyan genealogy? A very positive immediate response was received. Since then, I had been helping Dr. Mark G. Thomas in the collection of mouth swab from persons who claim their lineage of Sakyan clan and their non-Sakyan people.

Dr. Thomas has been instrumental in getting this project approved by the Joint University College, London/University College, London's Hospital Committee on the ethics of human research (study number 99/0196).

He had advanced the subject further, making it included in the curriculum as one of the papers in the study of M.Sc. degree in Human evolution and Behaviour, Department of Anthropology, University College, London. This latent study might show up first ever known to us.

Hypothetical reasoning of DNA, a nucleic acid that is the vital constituent of chromosome for transmitting genetic information in the form of genes from parent to offsprings. Our genetic material is organised into 46 chromosomes which forms pairs of chromosomes. In 22 pairs, the chromosome material is essentially the same, where one is derived from the mother of the individual and the other from the father, these pairs are known as autosomes. The 23rd pair of chromosomes is the sex chromosome, where the female has two X-chromosome, again one derived from each parent, but in the male, there are two very dissimilar chromosomes, the X and Y-chromosomes. The Y-chromosome in essence is the male determining chromosome and is only found in males. Thus, the Y-chromosome is paternally inherited, from father to son, generation after generation.

In the case of Sakyan, if their belief about a common origin, is true then we would expect the Y-chromosomes of different Sakyan population to be more similar to one another that they are to their non-Sakyan neighbours in all over the world.

This hypothetical test is under progress as the first step towards knowing the Sakyan genealogy, their way of migration and mutations.

Conclusion

In the annals of history a large number of ethnic tribes intermingled with nomadic Scythians who are living coextensively the whole of south-east Asia. They are visibly noticeable in many areas–yellow colour. They all originated from Central Asia, and it gives an inner strength of their own. They are divided by the provincial geographical areas of a nation—the world is divided into countries. Due to this an apportion of a some tribal groups are named separately and identified differently on basis of their spoken dialect and culture. Their genealogical lineage might origin from the same group but it has remained unknown, unclean or unestablished. As human memory is very shortlived, we forget the past very soon. As for example, the division of the Koch (Scythian) Kingdom in 1581 into Koch Bihar and Koch Hajo. Koch Bihar now has became a part of West Bengal and the Koch people intermixed with Bengalis and they are now a sect of North Bengal. Similarly, a Koch are with its population has became a part of Assam and their identity is as Assamese. Looking at Assam, we find that a Shan-Tai group of people who invaded Assam around 13th century intermixed with the natives and now known as Assamese. There are numerous group of people fell out from Shan-Tai Chou-lung-Su-Ka-pha in the year 1228 A D showed the seeds of Assamese nationalism Sunkapa's route of migration from Mou-lung in Yunnan to the river Brahmaputra across Naga hills and Patkas regions main line. The Sakyan in which Sakyamuni Gautama Buddha was born is one such generic group of Scythian Tribes from Central Asia. The genesis of Sakyan race has remained unknown. Modern geneticist are keen to make a study on this gruelling subject (hidden texture). The early history of Central Asia is closely related to the movement of people who appeared as early as paleolithic period. The Sakas are frequently mentioned in the long Indian history as Sakya in which Sakyamuni

Gautama Buddha was born. The Sakyan are now divided into many nations in south-east Asia. There must be some harmony, unseen characteristics in them. No study ever has touched on this subject with national thinking, what about the progenation of Sakyas? It is obligatory for us to develop thinking on this line. It would be very enthusiastic endeavour for modern science to unveil the mystery.

As a part to this matter, I hope, many would be joining hands soon.

Conclusion

We have studied "Conquest of Peace" in great detail. We have highlighted the need of peace and peace education. We studies the concept and the activities in detail. While reading these and simultaneously practicing in our hearts we have experienced peace within ourselves now, let us practice this art of being peaceful and happy. Modern society is conflict ridden within. Let us discover the treasure within. and lead enlightened life, full of values and free from anti-values.

Scientific Technology for Survival of Mankind

All challenges and threats facing mankind in the twenty-first century do not have their origin in the socio-economic-political aspects, but these are evolutionary in character. Physics has shown that all concepts (including all psychological imbalances), we use to describe nature are limited and finite, and are constructs of the mind; part of the map, not of the territory. We have divorced nature and have started living in a man-made social cosmos.

The acquisitive culture and the sanction for aggression benumbs sensitivity of the mind-brain-body system. Our involvement with the act of living—which implies energy transfer between the object (environment) and the subject (recalled memory)—has polluted our perception and conditioned the psyche over chronological time of psychosocial evolution. Historically, human evolution has deeply conditioned the psyche by an unbroken saga of challenge and response. And the conditioned psyche projects itself as pain, misery, sorrow and travails.

The psychodynamics of mind-brain-body system adds to entropy, which is leading to self-destruction and annihilation. Obviously this paradox cannot be resolved by reforms or treating the symptoms in the external world (time-space matrices). So, mankind has to fight the final battle of radical transformation (mutation) of the human psyche. We have to undertake a pilgrimage from scientific self-observation, to self-knowledge, to spontaneous action, and to harmonious relationship. It is a journey from fragmentation to homogeneity from partialness to wholeness from the movement of knowing to the action of understanding from the slumber of knowledge (information gathering) and experience to the state of being awake, to awareness. We are at a critical juncture when we have to understand the wholeness of life, which will bestow a quantum jump from psychosocial evolution to spiritual evolution. We have to construct the cathedral to spirituality on the foundations of science.

We urgently need a fundamental transformation in our thoughts, perceptions and values. We need a mutation of the very foundation of perception, the very source of response, the emergence of global ethics, and a few global order. A pure perception bestows intuition, which flowers into creativity.

Understanding comes only through self-knowledge, which is awareness of one's total psychological process. It deals with the Wholeness of Life, the Oneness of Life. It is ending of all psychological imbalances and bestows spontaneous equipoise and equibalance. We have to restructure education and science, so that these take into their ambient the Wholeness of Life. We have to deeply understand that all the 'inner movement' and the 'outer movement' are a single dynamic flow; it is a unitary process. It is a non-verbal communion between 'what is outside' and 'what is within'. It leads to a perception of the Wholeness or the

Oneness.

The mutation of the human psyche results in dimensional transformation, an entirely new way of living. All psychological imbalances go to abeyance and man revels in freedom peace and bliss.

Leaders from all over the world will go to New York in October 2000, for the 'Millennium Summit' to consider the challenges ahead and what the UN can do to face them. The present monograph is the 'first model' place before mankind and the United Nations. An approval of the monograph by the UN will ensure a close cooperation among enlightened persons all over the globe. Every country will open an institute for *Symboisis of Science and Spirituality* or *Inner Space Labs* or *Cartography of Inner Space to take up further research in this field.* This will become an individual and collective joint venture for human survival and excellence.

Preface

The last quarter of the twentieth century has led mankind to the final collapse of Cartesian-Newtonian thought structure and consciousness is now emerging as the fundamental governing our perceptions, our responses and our world model. The consciousness expresses itself in two dominant modes: (a) "the primacy of our inner conscious awareness as a causal reality", it constructs time-space-causation matrics in quick succession; and (b) to explore and understand the uncontaminated, unpolluted, unknown, eternal energy which pervades the whole of cosmos and beyond. It is also called the Intelligence, the Love, the Truth, the Supreme Reality, the Divine, the Universal Consciousness.

Man has started living in the man-made social cosmos, a construct of the conditioned mind-brain-body system a synthetic world, which is divorced from reality. The thrust of psychosocial evolution over uncountable aeons of time, has led to conditioning of the human psyche, a psychic pandemic. Mankind is at an evolutionary crossroads. We stand at a juncture wherein we are in supreme peril—not a peril from another species, not a peril from outer space but a peril from ourselves. From deep within the human psyche, there has developed this terrible power that threatens not only our generation but generations yet to be born, and not only our race, but all species of life on this planet.

The fundamental responsibility of the human race is to work for one's own survival and excellence. It is a challenge for our education and to our way of living. What the Buddha proclaimed about the imperative need to know the mind, to shape the mind, and to liberate the mind has been never more true than in the Age of the Atom. To know, to shape and to liberate the mind is only possible by scientific observation of the conditioned psyche, the flow of thought and its associated motivations.

We, as lovers of science, are learning to apply a scientific 'technology' to religion and spirituality. The foundation of scientific enquiry is rejection of an authoritarian approach, but an open-minded enquiry to understand the challenge in its fullness, so we have to begin anew and afresh. Maurice H. Wilkins, Nobel Prize in Medicine, 1962, wrote, "The open-minded enquiry of a scientist is not something peculiar to science itself but is a characteristic of the good way of living for human beings in general". The enquiry is to understand the wholeness of life in all its dimensions. B.D. Josephson, Nobel Prize in Physics, 1973, wrote, "Our nervous systems are designed to allow us to interact not only with the material level of existence but also with the spiritual levels." So our enquiry deals with interaction of conditioned mind-brain-body system with the environments and also interactions at the spiritual level.

Ilya Prigogine, Nobel Prize in Chemistry, 1977, wrote, "It is physics that presupposes an observe situated within the observed world. Our dialogue with nature will be successful only if it is carried on from within nature." Dialogue or experimental interrogation is only possible from within nature, which implies that the true subject is attentivity (awareness) and it sees the object (the fact); in this case there is no energy transduction between the subject and the object, and the subject has the awareness of the true object, the fact. Experimentation means the faithful observation of the true nature of the fact, or seeing the fact unrelated to our beliefs, our ambitions, or our hopes, or our desire. Experimental dialogue implies that nature reveals Itself (the attentiveness) to itself (the fact). J. Krishnamurti wrote:

> At the moment of attention all the conditioning disappears, all the image-building comes to an end; it is only when you are not attentive that the whole thing begins.

Attentiveness leads to dialogue with nature which implies that nature reveals itself as intuition or revelation or insight.

Insight is the timeless perception; it is perception of the wholeness of life. The perception blossoms into spontaneous action which gives true relationships. It is insight alone that can decondition the brain. Insight is complete and from that completeness there can be logical, sane, rational action. Only then there can be flowering of the brain.

Only then you have a complete relationship with the mind. Insight resolves all human challenges, all psychological imbalances. This is the consummation of human growth. Man revels in freedom, non-violence, peace, harmony and bliss.

Ours is a century dominated by science and technology. Many distinguished members of the world scientific community think that the destiny of mankind is largely determined by modern science and its offspring-technology. We have to explore where the present science and culture is leading us. Federico Mayor Zaragoza, in a Nobel Prize Winners Conference titled as "Facing the 21st Century: Threats and Promises", in 1988, spoke:

> Never before, until now, has the tension between science and the human conscience, between technology and ethics, reached a point where it has become a threat to the world as a whole.... We are so dazzled that we do not perceive the threats hanging over our heads, warning us of the pressing need for a radically new and universal ethical outlook on the future of present-day science.

The applications of science are at variance with profound and far reaching cultural requirements, principles of equity and interests of society. Bertrand Russell wrote that thanks to science and technology, mankind is united in evil but not yet united for good; that people have learnt the technique of mutual destruction, but not the more desirable technique of worldwide cooperation. Russell believed that wisdom becomes increasingly necessary with every advance in knowledge and technology, and that although our age has surpassed all others in knowledge, it has not enjoyed a correlative increase in wisdom; and he called for a "new moral outlook."

We know now, how to shatter civilizations, and

the knowledge will forever be with us. It is understandable therefore that, as the French sociologist Raymond Aron put it, the world is increasingly one of "virile weapons and impotent men". Martin Luthar King rightly said, "Science has completely finished our spiritual power, we have guided missiles but misguided men." We cannot base international order on such lethal behaviour, or on our present cultural belief structure. The notions of "common interests", "common security", and "common future" demands that uncompromising confrontations should be ended throughout the world and give way to harmonious existence. During the last 2-3 decades, an attempt has been made to seek behind all the conflicts a more universal perception of human dignity that is less subject to constraints of human history. Ilya Prigogine wrote that the last few decades of "the twentieth century have marked an irreversible turning point in the history of mankind—a turning point that heralds a new age, a bifurcation."

The aim of this monograph titled. "Pilgrimage to the Twenty-first Century" and subtitled "March of Psychosocial Evolution to Spiritual Evolution: A Scientific Vision" is further exploration of this turning *point*, which will result in a quantum jump from psychosocial evolution to spiritual evolution. This will usher an era of immediate perception, spontaneous action, and new relationship. This bestows non-violence and peace, love and compassion, delight and bliss. This implies a global spiritual renaissance which implies a new culture of freedom, non-violence, human values, peace and bliss in the next millennium.

Ervin Laszlo discussed the emerging concept of the cosmos in words:

The parts of this totality are not radically separate: they are integral elements of the whole. Every "thing" in the cosmos is a coherent "event" and every event is the summed result of all the other events. The cosmos is a system of interacting waves: it is a sea where the effect of the smallest perturbation propagates throughout the entire field .... the new physics and the new cosmology do not recognize discrete things and independent events in the universe, only ripples upon ripples, waves upon waves, interpenetrating and propagating in a seamless sea.

Everything in the cosmos is a coherent event and every event is the summed result of all other events. The observable world appears to have emerged from the "quantum vacuum (potentialities)" that constitutes the "ground energy state" of the universe. The ground energy state of the cosmos is the Eternity.

Life is a pilgrimage from womb to tomb. It takes the pilgrim, or explorer, or enquirer on an inner voyage of self-discovery from self-observation through self-knowledge to silence. It is a journey from fragmentation to homogeneity, from partialness to wholeness. The journey is characterized from pure perception to understanding, to spontaneous action, and to new relationships. A man grows from intellect to intelligence, from knowledge to understanding, from successive consciousness to awareness. That kind of psychic growth or mutation of psyche is necessary. It is a revolution, psychological revolution in which the whole human race has to participate. It is the global participation of the human being which is necessary.

We share the consciousness of all humanity, for our suffering, our pleasures, beliefs, conclusions, opinions, and all the religious dogmas and faiths are shared by all human beings on this earth. We live in a state of contradiction, and where there is contradiction, there must be conflict. We share the psycho-dynamics of mind-brain-body system, but the patterns of conditioning may be different. The basic challenge is to end the pollution of the human psyche. And if we do not radically transform our psyche, we remain more or less the same as we have been for thousands of years. In principle, the monograph deals with all human challenges facing man in the beginning of the next millennia and also presents an answer to the human paradox.

We have to explore pure religion or spirituality, which is a personal discovery of the meaning of life, uncovering the mystery behind the movement of relationship, discovering what it means to relate with Nature, man, organisms and environments. Religion or spirituality explores the wholeness of life. Spirituality explores: Who is going to observe and the state of the observer? What is that who is observing matter? It explores the observer and the observed, the interaction between the two? Who is 'I', the 'ego' ? It explores the quality of consciousness behind?; and What are the instruments of perception? It uses mind to explore the mind. In spiritual science, the emphasis is upon the act of perception, the quality of instruments employed for perception, the quality of consciousness behind the perception. Spirituality relates to personal discovery of the truth, the exploration of one's own subjective world. It is to transcend thought and cultural belief structure.

We have to explore a new non-violence, freedom, peace, relationship, democracy, justice and global governance.

Non-violence: Psychological violence implies the inward anger, hatred, wanting to dominate people, not only physical domination, but the domination of ideas. Psychological dependence, imitation, conformity, domination, all that is inward violence. Violence is an indication of psychological immaturity. All psychological imbalances—fear, greed, anger, acquisitiveness, search for security and so on—are different facets of violence.

Violence is a construct by symbolic-dualistic frame of reference and non-violence is a percept in the non-dual frame of reference of the mind spectrum; where the non-dual frame is synergistic or at higher quantum energy potential to symbolic-dualistic frame.

Freedom: It is not reaction, it is not choice. It is pure observation without direction, without fear of punishment and reward. It is without motive. Freedom is found in the choiceless awareness of our daily existence and activity. In freedom, there is pure observation, which is insight without any shadow of the past or of time. This timeless insight brings about a deep radical mutation in the mind. In freedom, there is negation of desire, pleasure, so there is love with its compassion and intelligence.

Peace: It is related to human psychology. As long as there is inherent violence in the individual psyche, the political leaders of the world and the Heads of States shall never be able to end war or create peace in the world. Peace is a total way of living. Peace requires the mutation of human psyche.

Relationship: Life is relationship—relationship to nature, to people, to society, to knowledge and ideas, to property, and to everything. The conditioned psyche always gives false, transient, ephemeral, finite relationship, so we have constructed a society which is beset with violence, fear, anger and other psychological imbalances. We have to self-educate ourselves—which implies to scientifically observe, to self-knowledge, and to insight or intuition. Understanding is direct perception which bestows insight. The aim of human life is to make a quantum jump from symbolic-dualistic frame to non-dualistic frame, from knowledge to understanding, from false relationship to true relationships. The truth comes into being only when there is a direct perception of it in your consciousness. Insight bestows a sense of love, affection, a sense of responsibility in our relationship. Insight teaches us to live harmoniously, live cooperatively.

A man has to grow from intellect to intelligence, from knowledge to insight (intuition), from self-awareness to understanding the wholeness of life, from successive consciousness to Simultaneous Consciousness. That kind of psychic growth is necessary. It is psychic mutation that is necessary. The mutation of human psyche blossoms into motivation of sharing rather than the motive of dominating and owning, in cooperation rather than security in property, in bank balance, in possession. The motivations of sharing and cooperation lead to freedom, peace and bliss.

True Democracy: Democracy is the government of the people, for the people, by the people. But the 'people', who expresses the wholeness of life is not there. Such a democratic society where every man acts as a mechanical golem, is bound to degenerate. The democracy cannot grow as long as man, which includes the society and the government, base the decision-making on past and dualism, and devoid of creativity.

The new dimension of true democracy is that all

decision-making must be made on perception of the fact, and not on mutilated fact, or the non-fact. A true democracy cannot function unless the absolute values of life of Truth (called spiritual values), love and compassion are inculcated in the minds of the people through education, cultural activities and socio-economic as well as political structure. The true democracy is based on non-dual frame of reference of the mind spectrum. We need a psychological revolution in which the whole human race has to participate and every man is an equal partner.

True Justice: Our society is founded on injustice, because every activity is governed by conditioned human psyche. No nation founded on injustice can grow and progress, but in the long run it is bound to annihilate itself. True justice flows from immediate understanding of life. It bestows equality and fraternity, food, clothing and shelter to all. It is only holistic education that helps man to grow from knowledge to understanding, from rationality to intuition, from intellect to intelligence, from confrontation to cooperation, from injustice to justice.

Global Governance: The encapsulating of time-space has reduced us to a global village or global cottage at physical level. Neighbourhood implies deep concern for the welfare of your neighbour which naturally implies deep concern for the human race. It leads to perception of brotherhood. All regional crises take the shape of universal crises and become the joint responsibility of the human race.

The global governance is defined as orderly management of our inner world and its reflection in the outer world. The global governance expresses a quality of life which carries creativity, spontaneity, so all actions are rational and lead to fulfillment. It is to live in communion with nature. Global governance flows from symbiosis of science and spirituality.

The Divine Law: The mind-brain-body spectrum functions predominantly in three modes: (a) *psychological mode*—all activity is destructive, leading to a great deal of misery, confusion and sorrow; (b) *scientific mode*—it explores the time-space matrices and gives relative knowledge; and (c) the *religious mode (meditative mode)*—it explores the universal core of religion, deals with the wholeness of life, and bestows absolute knowledge. We have to restructure the dimensions of science so that it takes in its ambient the 'inner world', so it must deal with the wholeness of life. We have to restructure education so that it takes in its fold the wholeness of life.

The Divine Law self-expresses itself when Universal Consciousness bathes every cell of the brain. The characteristics of the Law are intuition, spontaneity, freedom, love, intelligence, and so on.

The Divine Law or the Life is an adventure of Consciousness and Joy. It is the essential Truth of our Being, and Joy is its spontaneous expression. It self-expresses itself on the eternal and immutable planes of our Being. The Divine is defined as "An eternal child playing an eternal game in an eternal garden." Playing a game is the "Quest for its own Truth of Being", "A Quest for Joy", "A Quest for Delight", Love, Joy, Non-violence, Coherence, Oneness, Interrelatedness and Beauty are the fundamental determinate of the Divine Delight of Existence. These are the inherently embedded potentials of man. The Divine Self-expresses itself as hierarchical levels of Consciousness, or it is gradually manifesting itself at higher and higher quantum energy, potential, and in common parlance it is called evolution of man from psychosocial evolution to spiritual evolution.

The Divine Presence is the central Truth of our being and of all existence in the universe. The Divine Presence emerges out of inner peace and grows out of it without disturbing at all that perfect peace, which in turn gives it stability, and allows it to deepen eventually into bliss. The Divine Reality or the Divine Law is *Sat-Chit-Ananda.* Truth-Consciousness-Bliss.

Every individual has a direct and unique relation with the Divine, the Supreme, as it is determined by the matter content in the individual consciousness. Each one receives from the Divine what he deserves, when he is in a receptive condition. Therefore, from the psychological standpoint, everyone is all alone to have this direct relation with the Divine. This is the Truth which nobody can transcend. If you live the Truth of your being, you immediately have the unique and exclusive relation with the Divine.

Understanding: Man is born with two dimensions—self-awareness and understanding. In the common waking state, or symbolic-dualistic frame of reference, or relative frame of reference, there is self-awareness of the time-space matrices in quick succession, and thought coupled with its feelings and volition. In the non-dual frame of reference, the pseudo-subject (the recalled memory or thought-time) goes to abeyance, and true-subject (attentivity) takes over; it implies the entity, I-consciousness, the ego, ends. It bestows realization that the intellect, being limited and conditioned, is incapable of seeing the truth; this is the supreme realization for the intellect and realizing this it becomes silent and still. Total silencing of the intellect is the ending of the meditator (the pseudo-subject) and also of meditation (the entity, the 'I', the ego, which says 'I' must find God or Truth will never find it). Ending of the meditation is the flowering of love. When thought—time (consciousness, or intellect) becomes silent, the understanding self-expresses itself. Understanding happens when symbolic-dualistic frame of reference makes a quantum jump to non-dualistic, non-symbolic frame of reference in the mind spectrum.

J. Krishnamurti wrote, "Only the truth can liberate the mind from its own ideation; to see the truth, the mind must realize the fact that so long as it is agitated it can have no understanding... Stillness of mind comes only when there is no process of isolation through accumulation but complete understanding of the whole process of relationship.... In stillness there is no projection of thought." The understanding flowers into true democracy, true justice and true global governance. It also bestows freedom, peace and bliss.

The understanding flowers into right and spontaneous action and true relationship. It leads to a perception of the Reality, the Universal Consciousness, whose attributes are non-violence, fearlessness, freedom, peace and bliss. It leads to a way of living where there is no confrontation but cooperation, no competition but sharing, love and compassion between man and man, man and organisms, man and environments. It ushers a new realms of freedom, peace and bliss; it is to live in communion with nature.

The understanding of the Divine Law will lead to transcend the psychic age and be a harbinger to the spiritual age. This will guarantee human survival, progress, fulfillment and excellence.

Human Values: The conditioned psyche or man-made social cosmos constructs 'social values' or 'virtues', or 'moral values'. They are local, parochial and temporary in application. These are external relationships of the individual with society.

David Bohm suggests, "We are at present faced with the challenge of a breakdown in human values that threatens the stability of society throughout the whole world. I suggest that existing knowledge cannot meet this challenge, and that only insight can give rise to the sort of overall new approach that might meet it."

An ethical mind refers to non-dual frame of reference in the mind spectrum and it arises from the depth dimension of man. An ethical mind perceives the fact, the 'what is', it is also called the 'perception of the inner perceptual construct', 'direct perception of actual fact', an 'inward perception (i.e., through the mind)', an 'insight or intuition'; it gives 'spontaneous response', which bestows the capacity to meet the present challenge. The values are rooted in deep insight or intuition.

True ethics means, a movement from perception to perception. It implies self-expression of intelligence. Living ethically from moment to moment is practical and concrete, not as abstract idea. Ethics or human values arise from the depth dimension or from the spiritual dimension of man.

Value-oriented education brings awakening at all levels, so that the human potential is unfolded in its fullness. Value education has the capacity to transform a diseased mind into a very young, fresh, innocent, healthy, natural and attentive mind. The transformed mind is capable of higher sensitivity, and a heightened level of perception. This leads to fulfillment of the evolutionary role in man and in life. It has the capacity to jettison all psychological problems, including the mad armament race, fear of nuclear holocaust, ecological imbalances, violence, poverty, and hunger, and usher in an era of freedom, peace and bliss. It can create a new society.

No society can exist and progress without fostering ethical and spiritual values in its population. The survival of mankind is embedded in perceiving human values, in understanding the psychodynamics of mind-brain-body system, in understanding the science of life, and then living in the light of that feelingful understanding.

Universal and Eternal Religion: Every highly developed religion of the world has two dimensions—(a) historically conditioned socio-political expression of religion, which is local, parochial, transient, mutable, and deals with social customs; and (b) the universal core of religion which is non-local, infinite, immutable and eternal. The authenticity of the truths of the universal core of religion lies in their being perceived by spiritual experimenters and in their being capable of reverification by others.

The universal core of religion is a quest for discovering order in consciousness, or the inner world of man, or the search of truth that sustains man and all existence. Pure religion is also known as spirituality. This suggests that both pure science and pure religion are in search of truth, and are not antagonistic but complementary disciplines of life. The symbiosis of science and spirituality will produce fully integrated human beings and thus help to evolve a complete human civilization for which the world is ripe and waiting.

What we call Mind (with upper case 'M') is the non-dual frame of reference of Mind spectrum? The

Universal Consciousness expresses Itself in a non-dual frame as intuition, spontaneity, love and compassion, order and harmony. It is the first-hand personal acquaintance of the quantum jump of the conditioned energy consciousness to Universal Consciousness, or in other words, a quantum jump from fragmentary perception to the perception of the Wholeness.

The dynamic interply of science and spirituality is an inner voyage of self-discovery from self-observation through self-knowledge to Silence, the ultimate quantum energy potential of Universal Consciousness in a pure Mind. One travels from verbal knowledge to personal acquaintance with the wholeness of Life. The inner voyage ends all pain, sorrow and suffering, and ushers a new era of freedom, peace and bliss. It is learning in the stream of relationship, the mystery of the Wholeness, from successive consciousness to Simultaneous Consciousness. And this understanding and living in the light of that feelingful understanding is the key to human survival and excellence.

The Pilgrimage to the Third Millennium

The source of inspiration of the present monograph has been already published. *The Masterplan Paradigm for Human Survival and Excellence,* (1998, pp. 245-49); and *God in Science,* (1999, pp. 84-86). Swami Vivekananda, Sri Aurobindo, Divine Mother (Madame Mirra Alfasa), J. Krishnamurti, and other Indian Sages believed that the mutation of human psyche or quantum jump from psychosocial evolution to spiritual evolution, "the initiative can come from India and although the scope must be universal, the central movement may be hers". J. Krishnamurti wrote, "In India (spirituality) has been wiped out and destroyed. Yet it was therein India, waiting in the soil. Can we do something about it?" We intuitively believe that the central movement has already been initiated by Vimala Thakar and other living saints/sages in India.

Both Teilhard de Chardin and Sri Aurobindo foresee the coming of a new race and consciousness. Tagore, Lecomte du Nouy and Julian Huxley also had identical views Paul Davies concluded, "The laws which enable the universe to come into being spontaneously seems themselves to be the product of exceedingly ingenious design." John Wheeler predicted, "Some day a door will surely open and expose the glittering central mechanism of the world in its beauty and simplicity". Recently Vaclav Havel, President of Czech Republic, raised his powerful voice that "modern age (psychosocial evolution) has ended.... And something else (spiritual evolution), still indistinct, were (is) arising from the rubble".

We have to work for a global sharing, and evolve a global strategy to resolve the global challenge, preferably under the auspices of the United Nations. So the global action plan must emerge from the womb of modern science.

A Critique on the Challenges Facing Mankind

The threats and challenges facing mankind during the last few decades are terrorism, hijacking, religious fundamentalism, ethnic conflicts, organized crime, drug trafficking, corruption, pollution, population transfer, appalling brutalities, and so on. These are different facets of psychological violence of human psyche. We need to provide food, clothing and shelter to every human being in the globe. The triple crises of hunger, malnutrition, fear have to be resolved at a global level. All threats and challenges facing mankind are constructs of the conditioned mind-brain-body system, the diseased psyche, the psychic pandemic. The challenges are not political, nor economic, nor social, but are evolutionary in nature. Man is treating the symptoms through socio-economic-political reforms in the external field. This may lead to postponement of the crises, but it has no capacity to end the crises.

The challenge facing mankind can end only when the Universal Consciousness bathes the brain cells. It implies awakening of enormous energy (of Intelligence), radiating and integral to perception, which alone frees man from duality and bondage of time. This alone will enable man to view the world holistically and to hold and control knowledge and the technologies that threatens to overwhelm him. This leads to radical transformation of the mind-brain-body system and new relationships are expressed there—this is called *dimensional transformation.* Such a transformation bestows the reciprocity and mutuality, a compassion for the art of living with all human beings at the highest quantum energy potential of the Universal Consciousness. This jettisons all violence, fear, pain and misery from the globe and ushers a new era of freedom, non-violence, peace and bliss. So the individual, the family, the society, the Governments and the United Nations will have to work jointly for dimensional transformation or fundamental revolution.

Life is a mystery, it is Divinity, it is self-generated, self-sustained, and in our own body we can witness the dance of the Divine. Man is a miniaturized cosmos. Your tiny human form is a condensed cosmos—a field of innumerable hierarchical level of expressions of Consciousness. Harmonise them, manipulate them, get acquainted with them, and let them function coherently. We have to learn to live in the wholeness of life.

Awake, arise and unite yourself and Divinity, through the awareness of its presence. Remember the unity of life. Multiplicity is the outer form within the manyness, within the diversity. Unity, Oneness is the essence, because everything is interrelated.

Modern science with its powerful and precise language is now set to explore further. A new spiritual pyramid must be constructed on the present high intellectual platform. Science moves from the *without* to the *within*, and spirituality moves from the *within* to the *without*; both employ the technique of experimental observation.

We have to restructure our science so that it takes in its ambient the inner field and the outer field of man, which is called true science. When true science blooms, it is called spirituality or universal core of religion. True science explores the wholeness of life.

We have to restructure our educational pattern so that we are aware of the psychodynamics of our own conditioned mind-brain-body system which implies imparting self-knowledge. True science or spirituality or pure religion is a quest of understanding oneself, coming upon self-knowledge. We have to learn the art of living.

This monograph supplements *"An Action Plan for Human Survival"* in the book entitled *The Masterplan Paradigm for Human Survival and Excellence.* The ending of these challenges (or ending of psychological time) leads to mutation of the human psyche. It results in transformation of the very foundation of perception and the very source of response. This is the consummation of human growth. The awareness of the wholeness is the consummation of Intelligence, the Universal Consciousness.

We see a silver lining on the horizon. The whole of humanity is undergoing a psychological transformation and is, however, dimly, consciously aware of this. If man takes up the responsibility for mutation of his own psyche through understanding the psychodynamics of his own conditioned mind-brain-body system, then Nature, being benevolent, will assist man to heighten his awareness. The action has to be taken *here* and *now.*

Truth is a pathless land. It is a flight of the alone (non-dual frame of reference) to the Alone (the Supreme Reality). It is perception of the truth in that can bring mutation in the human psyche. The truth in a non-dual frame of reference self-expresses itself as intuition, spontaneity, freedom, non-violence, order and harmony, love and peace.

Resolution of Human Challenges

Our civilisation, which is entering the third millennium, is at a "nuclear and psychic crossroads" where it has to take the most important decision in history— "to be or not to be". It is for each one of us to decide whether to take the path of the Buddha (Wisdom) or the bomd (annihilation, destruction). The final battle for the survival of the human race has to be fought in the psyche man. The psychodynamics of mutation of the human psyche is embedded deep in the mind-brain-body system. We have to energise the inner Intelligence, the inner Healer and this ensures the survival of the human race. Let us prepare ourselves to be a fit recipient for the Divine Grace, which is always flowing in abundance. Nature is benevolent. Life is benevolent.

A quantum jump in the evolutionary march reflects a decision by Nature, which gets necessitated by the limitions of growth of one species. Quantum jumps implies a fundamental transition from a lower quantum energy potential to a higher quantum energy potential. This can only happen, when there is flow of energy from the Absolute, so, it is a resistanceless or frictionless or timeless flow. There is no place for human will or effort in this flow. Quantum jump is governed by Nature and not by human will. A quantum jump from psychosocial evolution to spiritual evolution of the human species is also a decision by nature which has become necessary because psychosocial evolution, left to itself, will lead mankind to extinction.

We intuitively perceive that invisible hand of Nature has started moving to set man's vision right: it has started working on jettisoning the "declining culture" and to express the "rising culture". The turning point has approached, we realize that evolutionary transformation of this magnitude—the transformation of psychosocial evolution to spiritual evolution-cannot be prevented by short-term socio-political-economic activities, and this provides our strongest security and faith for the future. The Truth or Consciousness or Being is enveloping and destroying the causes of the "fall of culture" and is slowly expressing itself as the "rise of culture", or it is now enfolding the outer and unfolding the Inner, or enfolding the explicate order and unfolding the Super-Implicate order.

We have to rise to the new perception of Reality. The survival of the human race and of our planet depends on the unfoldment of the tremendous spiritual energy—man has to prepare itself through holistic education to perceive and to live in that ocean of energy. The key to human survival in holistic education at all levels and at all moments. *The Action Plan* must be implemented, in all sincerity and truthfulness, *here* and *now.*

The survival of mankind and the survival of our planet is dependent on subjective scientists (enquirers, pilgrims, saints, sages), who permit Nature to express itself in a pure Mind, in a non-dual Mind. Nature or Truth or Love is self-referral; it expresses itself to itself. A consciousness with a new dimension, which is integral and all-inclusive in its nature, is the gateway to the last year of this century and the only guarantee for the survival of mankind and the planet. This is the *last call, last* opportunity to work for one's survival and excellence.

A Paradigm Shift of the Charter of the United Nations

Leaders from all over the world will go to New York in October 2000, for the 'Millennium Summit' to consider the challenges ahead and what the UN can do to face them. This will ensure a close cooperation among enlightened persons all over the globe. There appears to be an urgency to open a dialogue on this subject. Perhaps such an open dialogue may led to sharing our explorations on the subject. We have shared goals. It may be possible to share our insights with the scientists, educationists, philosophers-mystics, political leaders. We examine the monograph on priority with an open mind, as that will help to evolve a second model. It may also be possible to collaborate in this field with friends. We welcome critical comments.

The monograph is not written for specialists in different branches of science or for spiritualists, but for the layman. Each chapter is self-explanatory and penned for separate publication in different journals. The different chapters have now been compiled in this monograph. The occasional repetitions of argument are not oversights; they are mean to emphasise points where emphasis seems advisable and also with the aim that the reader may read any chapter he is interested in and each chapter must be complete in itself.

My contribution is naught as this is only a collection of 'flowers' from the great scientific truths and from the Supreme Truth (the Divine) harmoniously blended and presented as a bouquet. The conclusions are valid for all humanity and no sectarianism is inculcated. It is only an infinitesimal collection of the fragrance in the ambrosial hours of morning dew from the garden of the Lord, the Divine. It is my signature on a pattern of clouds, or on the ripples of a lake, or on the waves of the ocean. May the grace of the Lord be bestowed on humanity and all organisms.

I shall work on for Him, in Him, with Him, as he commands me. I will always do lovingly the best. I –the finite, transient and ephemeral–proclaim the wonder: Wonderful! Wonderful!! Wonderful!!! O Lord!

Appendices

Below are the two topics received from Bodhipriya Jaibharati, National Secretary, The Temple of Understanding.

Introduction

The statement in the preamble of the UNESCO Constitution, "Since war beings in the minds of men, it is in the minds of men that the defences of peace must be created" provides a guiding principles for this theme. Learning to be means to learn to live peacefully with oneself. Peace can be experienced within ourselves. Inner peace arises out of intrinsic inner richness, such as courage, scientific faith, scientific belief, scientific temper, love, friendliness goodwill, spirit of co-operation, love for common good and vision of truth, goodness and beauty, spiritual joy and wisdom. Peace is the result of wholesome living.

Peace as Resolution of Inner Conflict

Inner peace can be experienced through resolution of psychological conflicts. Conflicts are either external or internal. Most of our conflicts are internal within ourselves. According to Sigmond Freud, our mind is a battlefield where the life instinct is in conflict with the death instinct and with our super consciousness.

Self Knowledge

To solve our inner problems we have to learn to look within and observe how the mind works. The problems distressing the mind have to be perceived and understood. The more we understood ourselves, the more we mature psychologically, helping children to look within and understand the self is an important life skill. The gravity of this need in education is evident by the kind of immature acts people commit throughout their lives and throughout the whole world. Much disruptive behaviour of people arises out of their unresolved deep inner conflicts. Obviously one, who cannot live in peace with oneself, cannot live in peace with others.

Children's Spiritual Needs

Peace in one's life arises from the deep human spirit that underlines all faiths. Peace education deals with the depth of the human mind. Touching the seat of spirituality is necessary. Spirituality seeks for fulfillment through experiencing truth, goodness and beauty in the highest degree. It motivates us to seek about reality to develop discrimination about good and evil and to appreciate beauty and eradicate ugliness. The present education has failed even to recognize the need to promote education for human excellence. What can we expect from this system.

Children's spiritual needs are delicate and strong. They want to experience spirituality here and now. They want to enjoy truth, goodness, beauty, kindness, love, warmth, wonder, curiosity, fun, play etc. They want to feel secure and comfortable. Education should cater for these children's spiritual needs. UNO charter of the rights of the child makes it obligatory for the governments to satisfy such needs of the whole world. It is a pity that states have failed so far to satisfy this spiritual need of billions of children in the world.

Depriving them of such needs, surely withholds the blooming of their wholesome personalities.

Meditation: The Way to Self-Knowledge

Stephanie Herzog, an American teacher who

experiment meditation with school students, has recorded her experiences in a book titled *Joy in the Classroom*. She relates how children's imagination, listening, learning and the whole of classroom atmosphere, changed positively as children improved their meditation.

She says:

"Meditation is a technique in getting in touch with our inner wisdom. Most children grow up without ever discovering that there is a source of wisdom, strength and love, inside them. They look to their parents for these qualities but often parents are lacking in these qualities in themselves".

She reports:

"After using meditation in classes, I began to notice a definite change in the student's ability to be self-disciplined, self-motivating and responsible. It all just happened naturally.

The meditation Stephanie used included 5 steps:

1. Getting in touch with one's own self and relaxing.
2. Deep breathing to change and get control on emotions.
3. Concentration of mind.
4. Expansion of mind with imagination and intuition.
5. Grounding the new founded high-level awareness into a productive activity.

Imagination in Children

One of the secrets of a successful person is his capacity for imagination. Scientists, artists, architects, engineers, businessman, educationalists, etc., need vivid and clear imagination.

Creativity Comes from Imagination

Unfortunately many teachers discourage

imagination while over-emphasising realities of life and society. Taking away children's imagination would be depriving them from the joy of being children and to create. When their healthy imaginations are suppressed it may find other less healthy ways such as day-dreaming, self-enclosure, passivity, negative and anti-social behaviour.

Practicing Awareness

Meditation in true sense is an act of establishing awareness children have to be trained in being aware of dangers. Awareness is a survival life skill. Awareness brings, self-control composure and sharpening of attention.

The second level of awareness is being mindful of the movements of the body.

The third level is being mindful of the activity of the mind. When we are angry, we know that we are angry. We are carried away by our desire and illusions. Awareness helps us to overcome this inherent weakness of human mind.

Type of Meditation for Children

1. Go out to an open and a quite place. Sit quietly and listen to the sounds in the environment. This helps to develop awareness towards the surroundings.
2. Sit quietly and repeat in mind "I am a peaceful soul."
3. Watching a tree with a silent mind.
4. Looking at a flower and concentrating the mind on it. Dr. Zakir Hussian was very fond of this meditation. He used to meditate on roses in the Rashtrapati Bhawan. J.L. Nehru also meditation on roses, in Teen Moorti House.
5. Imagining a trip to the snow clad mountains,

valley of flowers, forests and flower studded parks.

6. Imagining a beautiful natural scene.
7. Sitting quietly and concentrating on breathing in and out.
8. Watching a young child playing and smiling.

Learning Activities

1. Walking Meditation. This is an activity about awareness, attention and soothing the mind. Children go out to an undisturbed place and walk up down freely. Some Buddhist Vihars in Sri Lanka have special narrow shallow and long pits in which sand is filled about one foot deep. Monks practice walking meditation in these pits. I practices it when I was a Buddhist Bhikshu in Sri Lanka during 1961.

2. Watching with Silent Mind. This activity is also about awareness attention and soothing the mind. It develops a spiritual relationship with nature.

Go out to a silent natural surrounding. Be alone with nature. Listen to the songs of the birds. Feel the freshness of the breeze. Enjoy the warmth of the sunlight. Awaken your love for the mother earth, trees, plants and the sky. Feel you are a part of the whole universe.

3. Learning to Relax. This is a stress releasing activity. Lie down on the floor, facing up in shavasana. Close your eyes. Focus attention on the whole body and say in mind:

I am relaxing my body.......... relaxing, deeply relaxing................

Start relaxing from your toes.

Tighten toes and relax them, let tension go.

Next focus on the muscles of the abdomen.

Next focus on the hands and chest.

Next focus on the neck and face.

Next focus on the muscles in the brain.

Tighten and relax all these.

Say in mind – I am relaxing, deeply relaxing. Stay calm and relaxed for some time.

4. Experiencing Inner Peace. This activity is about concentration of mind and turning the attention inward. Sit comfortably on a chair. Keep your back straight. Relax in body and mind. Calm down. Let the body settle down gradually in stillness and silence. Close your eyes. Feel all the sensations arising from the body. Now slowly focus on your breathing. Let breathing take place naturally and effortlessly. Concentrate on breathing in and out. Don't let your mind be distracted with other thoughts and memories. Concentrate on the start middle and end of each breath. This activity promotes inner peace and develops awareness and concentration Students develop and perform much letter by regularly practicing this activity.

5. Letting Go. This is an activity about stress releasing.

Lie on the floor comfortably. Relax deeply for some time. Once you feel relaxed say in mind, I am letting go the entire burden on my mind.

Recall all the worries, pronlems, fears and anxieties you have in mind one after the other. Feel it, accept it. Stay with it briefly and then stay: "I let go this worry briefly, completely and the mind is now relaxed and free." Do it until your mind is completely empty and free. Enjoy and experience the sense of release and the freshness.

It is an inmstant meditation we can use to bring back our mind to peace when we find ourselves disturbed or angry.

Concentrate on breathing in and out and repeat mentally:

"Breathing in I calm.

Breathing out I smile.

Dwelling in the present moment.

I know it is a wonderful moment.

Thich Naht Hans

7. Meditation on the Present Moment

This is an activity about living in the present moment. There is joy living in the present. Lie down in shavasana and realize that

"This is the present. I focus my whole attention on the present moment. Living is always in the present. This moment is new and fresh. It never comes again. Therefore it is precious.

Living in the present is so good, there is great beauty in living in the present moment.

Living in this present moment is joyous. This is a moment of happiness, contentment and peace.

When we have come in complete touch with the present moment we stop repeating and enjoy living in the present."

8. Meditation on goodness

We repeat calmly in mind until we really feel good. "Living is good.

Nature is good.

Everybody is good at heart.

Everywhere is good.

Every moment is good.

Everyday is in eternity.

I love life, I love all beings, I love the whole

Everyday is in eternity.

I love life, I love all beings, I love the whole universe.

9. Meditation on Sharing

This activity is about feeling for human brotherhood. Learn the following verse by heart and repeat it with loving kindness to all.

"Share in the suffering of others,
Delight in the joy of others,
Delight in the good fortune of others,
View the losses of others as your own loss."

Lin Ying Chang

10. Meditation on being Awake

This activity is about awakening. We repeat the following verse with loving-kindness soon after we awake in the morning.

"Waking up this morning I smile, twenty four new hours are before me, I vow to live fully in each moment and to look at all beings with eyes of compassion."

Nich Naht Hang

11. Controlling Our Anger

We repeat in our heart the following verse when we are angry until we calm down.

"Breathing in I know that anger makes me ugly.

Breathing out I do not want to be contorted by anger.

Breathing in I know I must take care of myself.

Breathing out I know loving-kindness is the only answer."

Nich Naht Hang

A List of Some Pillars Great Buddhist Monk

Shariputra, India
Ananda, India
Ashvaghosha (2nd century B.C.E.), India
Nagarjuna (c. 150-250), India
Xuan Zang (Tang dynasty of China)
Vasubandhu (c. 320-400), north-western India
Hui Yuan (334-416), China
Kumarajiva (4th, 5th century), China
Bodhiruci (5th-6th century), China
Luan Tan Luan (476-542), China
Ching Ying Hui Yuan (523-592), China
Chih Yi (538-597), China
Tao Cho (562-645), China
Hung Jen (601-674), China
Shan Tao (613-681), China
Saicho (767-822), Japan, originated in China
Atisa (982-1054), Tibet, originated in Bengal India.
Hiuen-Tsang, China who visited empire Harsha Bardhan's Court in 643 A.D.
Honen (1133-1212), Japan
Shinram (1173-262), Japan
Dogen (1200-1253), Japan
Han Shan (1546-1623), China
Hsu Yun (1840-1959), China
Susuki (1870-1966), Japan
Anagari Dhammapala (1864-1933), India
Tsong Kha Pa (1357-1419), Tibet

Chronological Table, Historical Developments (B.C.)

Dates	*Historical events*
B C 2500	(a) Members of Scythian Tribes Central Asia ran over west Asia and south-east Asia. 1800-1500 BC Aryans Came to India.
	(b) Members of Indus valley over ran eastward invading Punjab. The Vedas, ancient sacred literature were composed.
B C 1000	(a) Scythian reached Yun-nan (now in China), Tibet and Burma.
	(b) Members of Indus valley reached beyond Punjab and composed Upanishads.
B C 600	(a) Scythian reached the foothills of the Himalayas.
	(b) The Indian sub-continent was ruled by 16 (sixteen) great powers, be sides smaller independent kingdom, Sakyan kingdom was one of those tribal states.
B C 560	(a) Birth of the Buddha.
	(b) Sakyan clan already consolidated in Tibet andBurma.
	(c) To and fro movement of Sakyan clan from Burma to India and reversed from India to Burma during Buddha's life time.
	(a) Sakyan kingdom in Burma was surrounded by people belonging to Tai and Shan clan and ultimately their amalgamation has taken place.

B C 327	The invasion of Punjab by the great Alexander.
B C 322	The rise of Chandragupta Maurya.
B C 264	Accession of Ashoka.
B C 150	1. The stupas of Bharhut and Sanchi. 2. The Buddhist Philosopher Nagasena. 3. The Milindapanha (question of Milinda).

Buddhism Down the Ages:

C. 30 A D	The rise of the Kusana dynasty and they extended their power in India. The stupas in Sanchi.
C. 100 A D	Progress of Mahayana School of Buddhism.
C. 125 A D	Amaravati became an important Buddhist centre. It worth nothing the name Asvaghosa a leading Buddhist philosopher.
C. 185 A D	The Buddhist philosopher Nagarjuna.
C. 375 A D	The most splendid of the Ajanta Caves. The philosophers Asanga and Vasubandhu.
C. 630-644 A D	The Chinese pilgrim Hiuen-Tsang visited India.
C. 1200 A D	The invader Muhammadi Backhtyar Khilji (a Turki) destroyed and massacred Buddhism in India.

Bibliography

1. *Eastern Bengal District Gazetteers*, (Chittagong) Ls. S.S. Molley, 1908.
2. *Imperial Gazetteers of India*, W.W. Hunter, 1885.
3. *Myanmar Past and Present*, Vol. I, II, (1878) Lt. Gen. Albert Fytche.
4. *Mynamar from the earliest time to the Present Day* Sir. J.G. Scoot, 1924.
5. *Census of India*, 1891, Vol. III, C.J. O'Donnell.
6. *Journal Asiatic Society*, 1824 Harvey.
7. *British Rule in Burma*, Payre.
8. *Report on the Eastern Frontier of British of British India*, 1835 Captain R. Boileau Pemberton.
9. The Publication Division, New Delhi, 1957.
10. *Tribes of Burma*, Louis C.C.
11. A writing from Madam Adam Curie, London, a former advisor to the Pakistan Planning Commission.
12. *Monograph on Arakan Antiquities*, Dr. Forch-hammer, Soas London No. FNA.7/ 15536.
13. *Ancient India (A History of its Civilization), 1965,* D.D. Kosambi.
14. *Everday life in Early India*, M. Edwardes London, 1969.
15. *Hand Books for the Indian Army/ Races of Burma*, Maj. C.M. Eriquez, 1924 Soas No. 306/1870.
16. *Ethnography Principle in Practice*, Martyn Hammersley and Paul Atkinson London, 1987.
17. *The People of Asia*, 1977 Gordon T. Bowles.
18. *The Hill Tracts Between Assam and Burma and on the Upper Brahmaputra (1825)*, Lt. R.Wilcox.
19. *The Buddha and his Religion*, by Saint Hilaire, 1895.

20. *Census of 1891 Imperial series* Vol. IX, *Burma Report* Vol. I H.L. Eales.
21. *The Tai and Tai Kingdom, 1976*, Padmeswar Gogoi.
22. *Migration of Races in Burma*, F.S.V. Donnison.
23. *History of South East Asia*, D.G.E. Hall.
24. *A Description Account of Assam*, William Robinson.
25. *The Foundation of Buddhism*, 1998, Rupert Gethin, Oxford University Press.
26. *Footprints of Gautama the Buddha*, 1957, Marie Beuzeville Byles.
27. *The Awakened One*, 1994, Sherab Chodzian Kohn.
28. *Buddha*, Karen Armstrong, 2000.
29. The Social Organization in N.E. India in *Buddha's*, Richard Fick.
30. *The British Burma and its People (1878)*, Capt. C.J.F.S. Forbes.
31. *The Tribes of Brahmaputras Valley*, 1901, L.A. Waddel.
32. *Zen Theraphy* (1995), David Brazier, Constable, London, 1995.
33. *The Cambridge History of Southeast Asia Vol.* I from early times to C. 1800, edited Nicholas Tarling.
34. *Census of India, 1891* (General Report, J.A. Baisen).
35. *Census of India, 1901* (Burma) by C.C. Lowis.
36. *The Raiders of Arakan* (1971) by C.E. Lucas Phillip.
37. *The History of Hindustan* (translation from Persian) Alexander Dow, S. Beckert & P.A. Dhondt London in 1770, Reprinted Today and Tomorrow Printers & Publishers, New Delhi, 1973.
38. *Buddhism in Central Asia*, B.N. Puri Published, Motilal Banarsidass, 1987.

39. *A Descriptive Account of Assam*, by William Robinson.
40. *Buddha of Infinite Light*, D.T. Suzuki.
41. Shambhala Publication Boston and London, 1997, in Association with the American Buddhist Academy.
42. *Philosophy in India, Tradition, Teaching and Research*, Satchidanand Murty, Pullished by Indian Council of Philosophical, 1985.
43. *Language in a Plural Society*, 1998, edited, by chman M. Khubchandani.
44. *The Psychology of Nirvana*, Rune Johnson (1969), London.
45. *The Oxford Companion to Philosophy*, edited, by Ted Honderich, 1995.
46. *Buddha and Buddhism Myanmar the Life and Legend of Gautama, Rangoon*, Bigendet (P.A.).
47. *Sakya or Buddhist Origin*, Mrs. Rhysavidsd, London, 1928.
48. *Vision of Creation*, Eileen Conn and J. Stewart, London, 1995.
49. *Linguistic Survey of India* Vol. I, Part 1, Chapter V —The Siamese Chinese Sub-family by Motilal Banarsidass, 1927, 1973.
50. *They Simply Belong*, by Raja Tridiv Roy, Chakma Cheif.
51. *Encyclopaedia Britannica* 1973-74.
52. *An Outline of Indian Mahayana*, Eric Cheetham by The Buddhist Society, London.

Index

M

N

O